# CONTENTS

**ISBN :  978-2-37900-025-6**
**EAN :  9782379000256**
Legal depository : 3rd term 2023

EPISTEMEA
4 avenue de l'océan
56340 PLOUHARNEL, France
For all information, visit Howard's website
**howardcrowhurst.com** or write to epistemea@gmail.com

# VERSAILLES,
## THE OTHER STORY

### VOLUME 1 :
### THE SECRET SCIENCE OF THE SUN

## Howard Crowhurst

epistemea

2023

# INTRODUCTION

(1) The Château de Versailles at sunset.

The Versailles estate is an exceptional place. It's a dizzying array of monumental buildings, interior decorations of unique quality, breathtaking landscapes, gigantic water basins, hundreds of fountains, statues in every corner, some of them unexpectedly modern. None of this is flashy or bling, as we'd say today. We see a quest for perfection on a grand scale, but also in the smallest details. This place expresses a long-term commitment, a statement that is constantly adapted and corrected, giving the clear impression of a depository where ancient knowledge is passed on, steeped in mythology and inscribed in the omnipresent geometry and science of numbers.

When you're there, you hear tour guides constantly harping on about the fact that King Louis XIV had a huge ego, which explains the incredible extravagance of Versailles. Of course, none of these guides has ever been king of a country, and can't imagine the psychological pressure of such a situation. They also forget that Louis XIV had a very difficult childhood. He almost drowned and had 4 very serious illnesses, the last of which was typhoid, which he contracted at the age of 19. The doctors said he would die. He received the last rites before miraculously recovering.

Furthermore, his childhood was punctuated by great political tensions, periods of flight and exile during the Fronde, when the French parliament was seriously questioning royalty. Finally, he was forced to marry a Spanish princess he'd known for only 3 days, in order to end the war with Spain.

When he was crowned King of France on June 7, 1654 at the age of 15 in Reims Cathedral, Louis XIV must indeed have had a strong character. But a king doesn't share his inner world, for he must ensure the stability of the kingdom through his personal stability. The king's life is a symbol, and does not take place in the same space-time as that of ordinary people. His actions should therefore not stem from his ego, but encompass a higher dimension. Louis XIV was well aware of this, as we can conclude from his last words:

*« I am leaving, but the State remains. »*

He didn't really have time to immerse himself in the royal ways of his father, Louis XIII, who died when he was just four and a half. Of course, we know a number of people who must have strongly influenced him, but do we really know everything? Could there have been secret influences in his entourage? Numerous elements present at the Château de Versailles tend to confirm this.

This is the subject of this book.

Why would there be a secret history at Versailles? What would one want to hide? For many years now, I've been trying to understand the real history of mankind on Earth. This quest began with my studies of the megalithic monuments around Carnac in Brittany, the first of which date back 7,000 years, and which don't fit in at all with the image we have of "prehistoric" man of that era. While there was clearly an advanced civilization that pioneered megalithic architecture, with countless menhirs standing in rows for miles across the countryside, we have no memory of it.

I have come to the conclusion that there is a universal law which means that we can only access a small part of the truth, perhaps only a tenth at most. The examples are numerous and very well known. We only use 10% of our brain (on a very good day). 90% of our DNA has an unknown function. We can only perceive 10% of the entire mass of the universe. And perhaps worst of all, we only remember a tiny fraction of our own lives. Apparently, it's all recorded in our subconscious, but we can't access it.

We popularly call this phenomenon "the tip of the iceberg". What appears in our visible field is only a small part of a huge thing that lies beneath the surface. Of course, we can apply this same principle to our personal lives. We all have our own secret garden, a way of seeing and thinking that we find impossible to share with society. We tell ourselves that it's of no interest to anyone, or that we don't want to disturb anyone, or that it would be too dangerous for us to reveal ourselves, but the reality remains that our secrecy occupies a good part of our existence. We may or may not be aware of it.

Does the law of the iceberg extend to history? Could it be that we only know the superficial part of our past? Could it be that much has happened on this planet that we know nothing about? I don't mean to evoke the conspiracy theories we hear so much about these days. Rather, I'm suggesting the existence of a universal principle that pervades our nature and makes it impossible for us to share our depths, whatever our justifications for doing so. And since our society is made up of individuals, personal secrecy is multiplied when it comes to recounting our shared past.

By force of circumstance, I've specialized in being an iceberg "finder". I'm beginning to recognize the little bits that stick out and indicate the presence of something underground. So sometimes I start to dig a little and uncover things that don't fit in at all with our vision of reality. I come to realize that there are little bits sticking out everywhere.

In this case, I decided to poke around the Château de Versailles, one of France's symbols of greatness. Officially, the Château was originally a small hunting lodge built by Louis XIII, who decided to turn it into something a little more substantial because it was convenient for him to hunt between Saint-Germain-en-Laye and Marly-le-Roi. He found it pleasing, one thing led to another, and the château became something more substantial. Later, his son Louis XIV developed the town of Versailles and moved the entire court to the château.

But what did Louis XIII like about it? Why would the king have chosen this particular location? Was it a decision he made on his own, or was he influenced by someone? However, the main question that came to my mind was...

**"Why did he orient his château and gardens the way he did?"**

Because everyone thinks about the orientation of their future home.

One main criterion is exposure to the sun and light. There's also the question of view and, for the average person, alignment with the street, neighborhood and access. It's quite likely that for a king there are other factors influencing his decision. If he's a good king, his main concern is the good of his country and his people. According to the French Wikipedia page on the Grand Canal at Versailles:

*We sometimes read that every year, on September 5, the anniversary of Louis XIV's birth (in 1638), the sun sets in line with the Grand Canal; other sources mention August 25, Saint Louis Day. In reality, neither of these statements is correct: it's only on August 16 (and April 26 in spring) that such a sunset can be observed.*

We are referred to a footnote which states:

*Azimuth of the Canal [291.9°] measured on https://www.geoportail.gouv.fr/carte [archive]; azimuth of the sunset calculated from https://www.sunearthtools.com/dp/ tools/pos_sun.php [archive]. As the Gregorian calendar is not perfectly aligned with the tropical year, from one year to the next the sunset on the axis may occur one day earlier or later than the dates indicated.*

Obviously, the best way to know the date of a sunset is by observation over several years, which does not seem to have been the case for the person who wrote this article. The text continues with the following sentence :

*The history of the construction of the park at Versailles suggests that the orientation of the canal was simply determined by the topography of the site.*

What if not one of these explanations were true, but rather both?

What I will try to show you in this book is that the place where Louis XIII decided to build what was to become one of the most important palaces in the world, had very particular, not to say unique, characteristics. It is even possible that these features had been recognized long before Louis XIII decided to settle there, and that his actions were in response to a destiny he agreed to follow, and which would involve France in its entirety. I would suggest that Louis XIV was aware of this project and decided to pursue it, following in his father's footsteps, as the axis of the Grand Canal strictly follows that laid out for the Château, the gardens and the fountain called Bassin d'Apollon by Louis

XIII from the outset. We shall see that Louis XIV's installations were inspired by a very ancient science, maintained in part in China under the name of Feng-Shui, but secretly known in the West since Megalithic times. Part of this science was known in the Middle Ages under the name of Quadrivium. In order not to burden the text of this book with the details of this science, which is nonetheless indispensable to understanding the layout of Versailles, its water features, its groves and its gardens, I have decided to write it in two volumes; the first is an introduction to the subject, some glimpses of the unspoken history and a presentation of the principles of astronomy and the calendar. The second will reveal the measurements, geometry and numbers that went into the development of this project. I have also decided to create a number of appendices at the end of each volume in which the reader can consult the calendrical, astronomical, numerical, geometrical and metrological principles that were obviously used in the selection and layout of this site.

It will become apparent that the name "Sun King", attributed to Louis XIV at a later date, despite Charles Perrault's claim that "His Majesty having taken the Sun for his motto", is part of a staging process that fits in with this destiny. I hope to be able to pull back, if only a little, the veil that hides the 90% of the truth according to the law of the iceberg I mentioned earlier.

# Louis XIII's Heritage

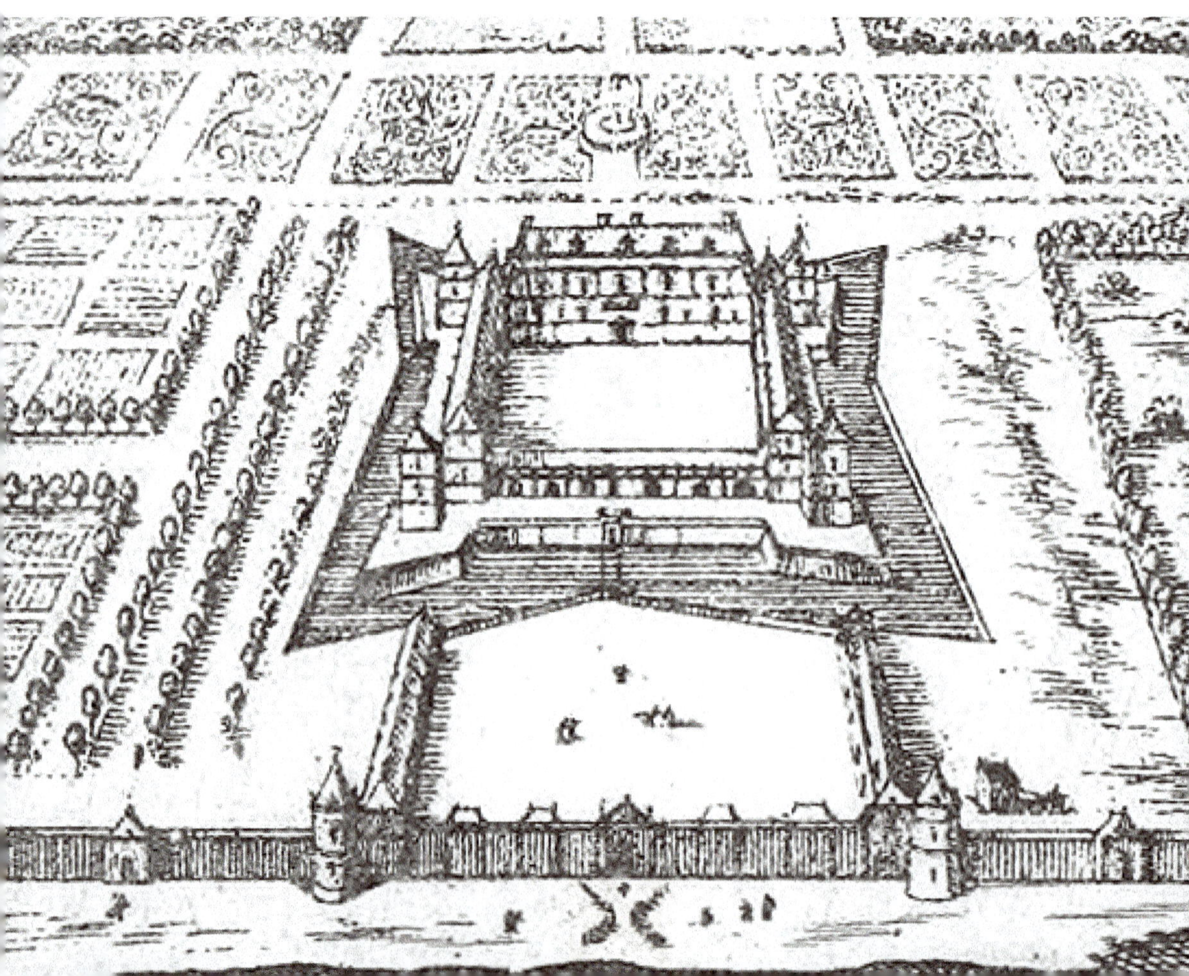

he generally accepted view of the Château de Versailles is that Louis XIII played only a minor role in its construction, and that Louis XIV is really responsible for its importance. This idea is strongly challenged in a superb article by Jean-Claude Le Guillou in Versalia magazine[1].

*"In itself, Louis XIII's Versailles estate was relatively small. However, as fate has placed it at the origin of one of the most prestigious gardens in the world, the story of its creation certainly merits detailed study. Louis XIV certainly deserves the glory of having magnified the gardens of Versailles, and Le Nôtre the prestige of having responded to royal desires by imagining prodigious earthworks and inventing a thousand surprises in the bosquets; but all these marvels were part of a pre-existing master plan, which had been desired by Louis XIII and drawn up by his gardeners Jacques Boyceau, Jacques de Menours and Claude Mollet. It was they who had definitively set the course for the future of Versailles by determining the general orientation of the gardens, distributing the network of paths, imposing the proportions of the bosquets and deciding that the gardens would begin with a parterre spread out in front of the château and end with a sumptuous stretch of water shimmering in the distance".*

This text therefore affirms that the principles for the layout of the château and gardens were firmly established by Louis XIII and his advisors, right from the start of construction in 1623 (2).

Of course, before these buildings were built, the choice of location had to be made, and the least we can say is that this choice did not correspond to the usual criteria. Louis XIII's first château was built on a hilltop topped only by a windmill, as the site had a reputation for being very windy.

Its occupation had been abandoned by the inhabitants of Versailles following repeated storms that destroyed their buildings. But the difficulties didn't stop there. At the

---

1     Jean-Claude Le Guillou, *Le domaine de Louis XIII à Versailles*, Versalia n° 3, 2000

foot of the hill was a place where all the water from the surrounding hills and a stream, the Val de Galie, flowed together. Together, they formed an unhealthy swamp. The area was so dangerous that during the drainage and development work carried out by Louis XIV, over 3,000 workers died of malaria!

It was here that Louis XIII decided to build his first "small" château, with the same orientation as today's(3).

Now, we give no "meaning" to this orientation.

***"And yet everything had come about without preconceived design.** First there was a simple house, then a first park and then a second, which were successively juxtaposed on three occasions, in 1623, 1627 and 1631, according to the Versailles estate archives. These somewhat forgotten archives have scarcely been exploited to the full extent of their merit, yet they reveal in great detail exactly what Louis XIII's estate was and how it was formed."[2]*

And so, one of the most imposing palaces of all time was implanted "without preconceived design".

This little phrase is what I call the tip of the iceberg, a kind of anomaly that doesn't fit with the context. It's the logic of a commoner applied to the decision of a monarch. We need to understand that Louis XIII felt himself to be an intermediary between Heaven and Earth. His life was part of destiny. A tiny phrase, his slightest action could have incalculable repercussions, and he must have been aware of this. If we don't know the reasons behind this choice of direction, it's simply that we weren't informed; that doesn't mean there wasn't a reason. We can't imagine that King Louis XIII's château could have been built "off the cuff". A cursory examination of the site's topography shows that this first château was built perpendicular to the valley formed by the Val de Galie (4). Being on the highest point, the chateaux's view was directed westwards towards the setting sun along this valley. This topography is clearly visible in old engravings, and is even perceptible today. A current topographic survey clearly shows how the great Versailles basin is situated at the bottom of this valley, oriented along its axis.

From the top of the castle hill, there's also a fine view in the other direction, towards a more wintry sunrise.

As we can see, the first castle seems to have been built according to the topography and the view, and we could stop our investigation there.

But why this location? Is there something breathtakingly remarkable about the view?

To understand this choice, let's take a closer look at Louis XIII's personality.

---

2       Idem

(4) Next pages: Cavalier view of the Château de Versailles in 1668 by Pierre Patel. The axis of the valley is obvious.

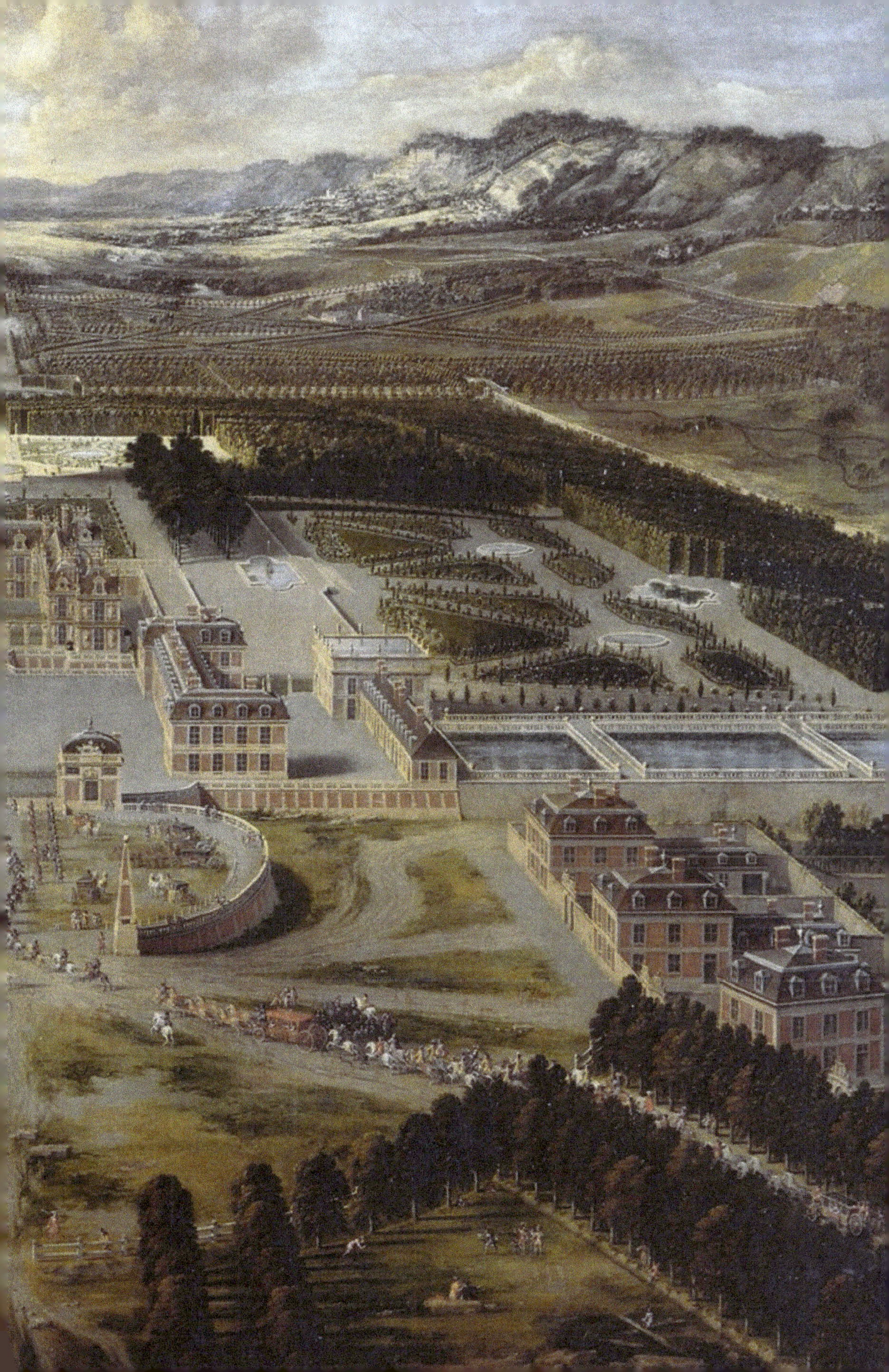

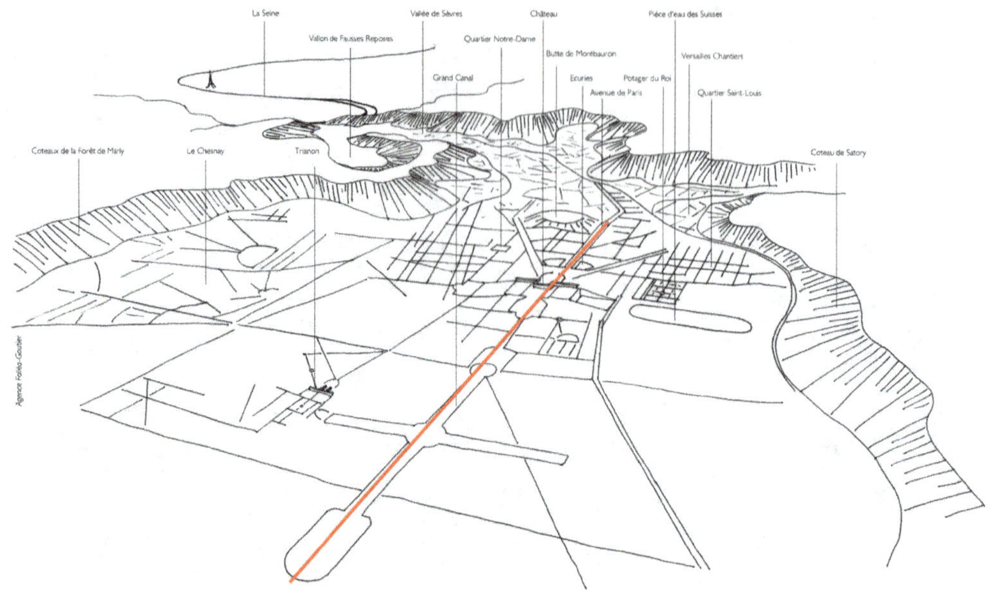


(6) Topography around the Château de Versailles showing the orientation of the Val de Gali (Versailles Tourist Office drawing).

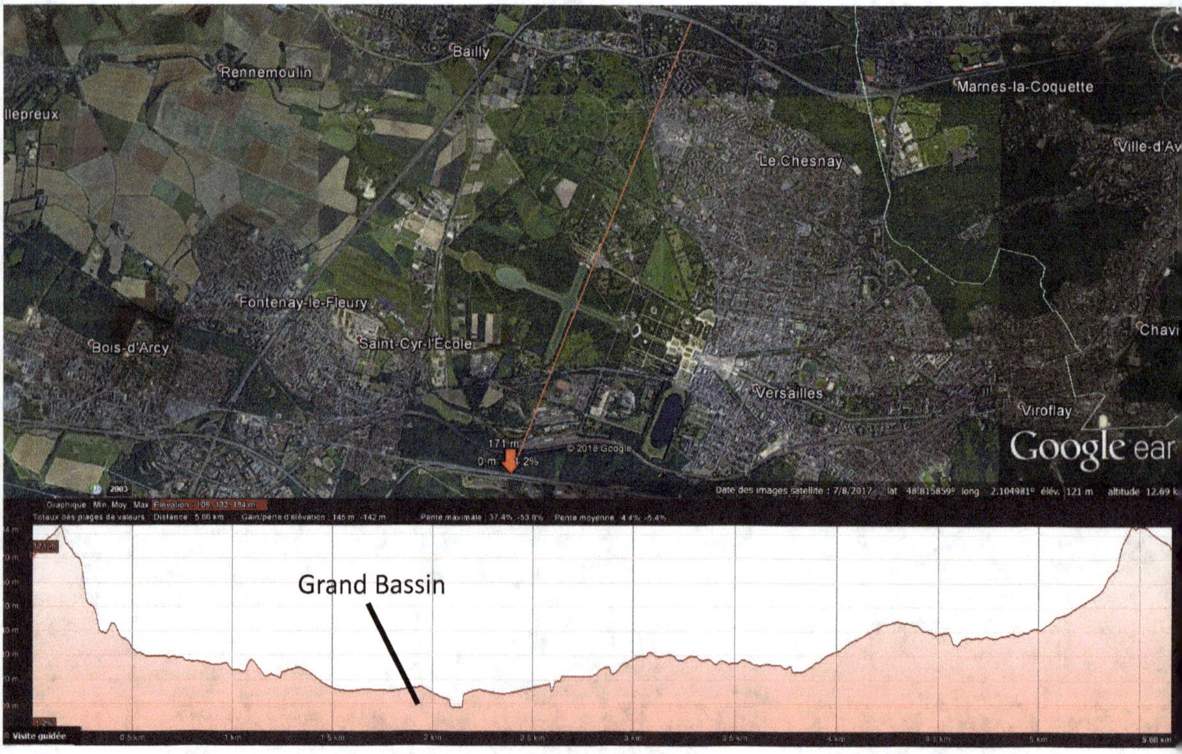

(5) Cross-section of relief along the red line with the Great Basin.

# LOUIS XIII, THE VIRGIN MARY AND AUGUST 15

A well-known feature of Louis XIII was his great religiosity, his devotion to Catholicism, which earned him the title of Louis the Just. Despite his supreme position as King of France, however, Heaven did not seem to favor him, for a terrible reality was tarnishing his existence. Since his marriage to Anne of Austria in 1615, the couple had remained childless. There was no heir to the throne. The situation was becoming increasingly alarming as the years went by, and as a result, the number of intrigues and plots grew. All the nation was worried.

To remedy the situation, the King turned to religion.

Between 1632 and 1638, Louis XIII made a series of promises and acts of devotion to the Virgin Mary in order to secure an heir with his wife Anne of Austria.

He had long been a member of the Confraternity of the Blue Penitents, inspired by the life of St. Francis of Assisi, the values of which were poverty, joy and love of divine creation, prayer and evangelization. In 1622, he laid the foundation stone for the new Blue Penitents chapel in Toulouse (now the Saint-Jérôme sanctuary). On October 26, 1632, he came there with his wife, and, from the royal rostrum, made a solemn vow to the Virgin in order to obtain a successor to the Crown of France. Later, in 1637, he made public displays of devotion to the Virgin at various locations in France, creating, for example, a perpetual lamp at Notre-Dame Cathedral in Paris.

According to Wikipedia :

*On October 27, 1637, a monk, Brother Fiacre, while praying, received an inner revelation: Queen Anne of Austria was to publicly request three novenas of prayer to the Blessed Virgin at the Church of Notre-Dame-de-Grâces in Cotignac (Var), and a son would be given to her. Informed of this prediction, Anne of Austria continued the novenas begun by Brother Fiacre on November 8, 1637. The novenas were completed on the following December 5. Exactly nine months later, on September 5, 1638, Louis-Dieudonné was born at the Château Neuf in Saint-Germain-en-Laye.*

The Queen's first pregnancy at the age of 37 was seen by the King, and subsequently by the whole nation, as a miracle granted by the Virgin Mary.

*On February 10, 1638, Louis XIII decided to consecrate the kingdom of*

*France to Notre-Dame. This was the famous "Vow of Louis XIII", in grati-tude for the pregnancy of his wife Anne of Austria after twenty-three years of marriage. With this vow, Louis XIII introduced the processions of August 15, during which his subjects were to pray to God and the Virgin Mary for the King's success. In addition, every church in the kingdom was to dedi-cate its main chapel to the Queen of Heaven, if the church itself was not under the patronage of the Virgin.*

It was at this point that August 15 became a national feast day, leading later to the introduction of a public holiday.

There can be no doubt, therefore, that Louis XIII had a special devotion to the Virgin Mary, and consequently to August 15, which must have been a very important date for him.

(7) (LEFT) PORTRAIT OF LOUIS XIII IN MOURNING COSTUME BY FRANS POURBUS LE JEUNE (PAINTING PHOTOGRAPHED BY JEAN-POL GRANDMONT).

# THE «AIM» OF VERSAILLES

(8) (below) Sunset on August 15 at Versailles (by Google Earth).

With these unusual facts in mind, we can return to our question about the orientation of the Château de Versailles, decided by Louis XIII. An astonishing fact challenges the established image of this place.

**The Val de Galie is oriented exactly towards sunset on August 15.**

The natural topography creates a kind of viewfinder that orients the entire landscape towards this date (4). The orientations of the first château, established in 1623 - 15 years before Louis XIII's vow - and subsequently extended to the entire park, including the gardens of Versailles and the Grand Canal, rigorously follow the axis of the August 15th sunset.

The precision of this orientation is perfect, as can be seen in the sequence of photographs taken on the axis behind the Apollo's Fountain on August 13, 14 and 15, 2018 (8). This axis is offset from East to West by 21.8°, an angle that is far from insignificant.

However, this offset is never given. The official Château de Versailles website states:

*André Le Nôtre organized the gardens of Versailles around two axes, north-south and east-west. The first runs from the Neptune Fountain up the Water Walk to the Orangery and the Lake of the Swiss Guard[3]. The second, called the Grande Perspective[4], crosses the gardens like an axis of symmetry, beyond Latona's fountain, following the Royal Way to the Grand Canal. Optical effects and surprises are characteristics of the French garden, which the King's gardener masters to perfection and employs at Versailles, notably in this perspective.[5]*

While this text highlights the subtlety and finesse of these magnificent layouts, it completely misses the "aim" of these alleys. It ignores the topographical, calendrical and astronomical foundations on which everything was built, giving the wrong orientations. While we speak of two axes, north-south and east-west, these announced orientations are approximations, a way of naming them.

They do not correspond to the true cardinal directions.[6]

---

3    In red on inside cover plan.

4    In blue on inside cover plan.

5    https://www.chateauversailles.fr/decouvrir/domaine/jardins/allees#lallee-deau

6    Voir "Appendix 1. Equinoxes and cardinal axes.", page 112

August 13

August 14

August 15

August 13
August 14

August 15

Unintentionally, they mislead the reader.

Here's a fact that begins to reveal what is hidden under the tip of the iceberg. This axis is most likely the real reason for the choice of this location and the establishment of this château.

**After all, it's no secret that the Versailles axis is linked to solar symbolism.**

It's clear that the Apollo's Fountain, where Apollo's chariot is positioned at the very center of Versailles' major axis, confirms the solar principle of this axis. Contrary to popular belief, this fountain was built as early as the time of Louis XIII.

*"Here, to collect water as much as to provide a visible decorative feature of the château, Louis XIII had a vast reservoir dug, which was given the shape of a sumptuous four-lobed pool measuring 60 rods (117 m) by 40 (78 m)[7]. Between 1633 and 1655, this pool was commonly referred to as "le canal", and in 1650 Fréart de Chambray gave it the name of "Rondeau", followed by "pool of the swans' fountain" and finally "Apollo's pool", as it still is*

---

7     60 to 40 is a ratio of 3 to 2. We will come back to this geometry in the second volume, as the value of the rod is given here ast 1.95 m which is 5 x 0.39 m. Let's just note here that 117 = 3 x 39 and 78 = 2 x 39.

*today. To create this water feature, which had not been foreseen in 1631, and to add some space around it, the park had to be enlarged by taking a rectangular area of 3.5 arpents (1.5 ha) from the "fief de Musseloup". This was done around 1632 or 1633.[8]»*

Later, in 1670, the statue of Apollo's chariot was installed by André Le Nôtre.

*«It represents sunrise. Because of its location on the grand perspective and its solar iconography linked to the very image of the Sovereign, this fountain is of great importance within the garden layout."* [9]

Despite what is stated in this quotation, if Apollo pulls the solar chariot from west to east, this is rather the sign of the setting Sun, for while during the day we see the Sun progressing from east to west, at night the invisible Sun returns from west to east below the horizon, to rise the next day in the east. Perhaps that's why the chariot is in the water: according to ancient tradition, this journey takes place under the ocean, which lies to the west.

However, the date of sunrise on this axis is far from insignificant, as it is **November 1st**, also a public holiday in France. King Louis XIV's bedroom opens in this direction, as does the entire structure on the east side of the château, which is like a parabola (33). The origins of this holiday are much more ancient than is generally accepted, and we'll come back to this later ("The Celtic calendar at Versailles", page 48).

For now, let's point out that these two dates, August 15th and November 1st, are symmetrically placed around the autumn equinox, 39 days before and after September 23rd.[10]

In Louis XIV's château, one of the most striking rooms is the Hall of Mirrors, built by Jules Hardouin-Mansart between 1678 and 1684. A total of 357 mirrors are installed under its 17 arcades, with 21 mirrors (3 wide and 7 high) per arcade.

Under the rounded ceiling, Le Brun's paintings (13) are organized around a central painting that Racine entitled The King governs by himself (17), a painted phrase that sits exactly above the gallery's central arcade, with 8 arcades on either side. As a result, it is

---

8  Jean-Claude Le Guillou, idem, p.102

9  Pierre Lemoine, *Versailles, Château domaine collections*,  1991 p.231

10  See «Appendix 5. A Druidic influence at Versailles?», page 127 on the solar chariot and the Grotte de Téthys, installed in 1666 on the site of the present-day north wing of the château, according to an idea by Louis XIV, and which represented the resting place of Apollo and his horses after crossing the sky by day, i.e. after sunset.

# Sunset on August 15 at Versailles

(10) (opposite, top) From the Water Parterre in front of the château in 2020. Hundreds of people watch the Sun set in the main axis of Versailles during the Grandes Eaux Nocturnes, unaware of the significance of this event. The water jets point towards the Sun, like ephemeral obelisks.

(11) (opposite, bottom) From the Hall of Mirrors balcony in 2019. Due to the difference in height between the Apollo fountain and the château floor, sunset is slightly offset to the right (north).

(12) (below) In the axis of the Dragon Fountain in 2020. The Sun descends into the open mouth of the sea monster.

perfectly aligned with the Grande Perspective, the central axis of the western gardens (14).

In fact, all these mirrors face the August 15th sunset, whose light enters through the windows opposite the mirrors, bathing the whole room in the glowing light and special energies of that moment.

Once again, we need to understand that all these mirrors were installed in this precise location to amplify the tribute to the Virgin Mary, protector of France, and without whom Louis XIV would never have seen the light of day!

*The painting The King governs by himself depicts Louis XIV in person, combining allegories and the gods of Fable. The king is in the center, seated on his throne, the tiller of state in his right hand. Yet the allegori-*

(13) (OPPOSITE PAGE) THE HALL OF MIRRORS WITH ITS MAGNIFICENT CEILING PAINTED BY LE BRUN.

(14) (OPPOSITE) THE GRANDE PERSPECTIVE CAPTURED IN THE MIRROR BELOW THE PAINTING "THE KING GOVERNS BY HIMSELF".

(15) (BELOW) THE HALL OF MIRRORS DURING RUSH HOUR.

*cal nature of Le Brun's paintings makes them difficult for the uninitiated to understand. The recent restoration of the Hall of Mirrors at Versailles, completed in 2007, has led to a breakthrough in understanding, following the discovery and deciphering of the gallery's earliest inscriptions, written in Latin, which had previously remained completely unknown beneath the French inscriptions still in place.*[11]

The first inscription in the central painting was by François Charpentier (after le Mercure galant, January 1685):

*Louis the Great in the flower of youth, takes in hand the helm of the State, and renouncing ease and pleasure, gives himself entirely to the love of true glory.*

This inscription was replaced by the one by Boileau and Racine (after Rainssant 1687):

*The King takes on himself the management of his States, and gives himself entirely to affairs. 1661.*

The final inscription, *The King governs by himself, 1661*, replaced this one.

It's interesting to see the evolution of these inscriptions. The first refers to the young King's renunciation of pleasures, a kind of sacrifice of ordinary earthly joys in order to achieve true glory. In our time, the pursuit of glory is seen as fundamentally selfish. Here, the opposite is true. However, this "true glory" becomes "'affairs", and takes on a distinctly earthly connotation.

What is behind these changes to the inscriptions? Could it be that the King's entourage has lost touch with the idea of his "solar" nature, i.e., non-egotistical and above the common man?

Let's now summarize the facts presented in this chapter, which should change the way we think about Versailles.

1. **As early as 1622, Louis XIII had the foundation stone laid for the Blue Penitents chapel in Toulouse. Ten years later, he came to the chapel with his wife to make a solemn vow to the Virgin Mary in order to have an heir.**

2. **In 1623, Louis XIII determined the layout of the château and gardens at Versailles.**

---

11      Text adapted from Hall Bjørnstad *« Plus d'éclaircissement touchant la grande galerie de Versailles » : du nouveau sur les inscriptions latines [*]* In Dix-septième siècle 2009/2 (n° 243), pages 321 to 343

3.  **On February 10, 1638, Louis XIII consecrated the kingdom of France to Notre-Dame and introduced August 15 processions throughout France.**

4.  **The orientation of all the gardens and the Grand Bassin de Versailles is perfectly aligned with sunset on August 15.**

5.  **The solar nature of this axis is well known to all specialists through the presence of the fountain of Apollo's chariot, itself likened to the Sun.**

6.  **No connection has yet been made between these different facts. Thousands of visitors can watch the Sun set on the Versailles axis on August 15 without receiving any information whatsoever.**

These facts can be seen as embarrassing. If the Versailles solar axis is obvious to all specialists, as we've seen, why wasn't this taught at school? How is it that no one has talked about this before, and that there are no photographs of it in books? Is it a secret or simply ignorance? Why didn't Louis XIII or Louis XIV or their commentators mention this fact, which must have been fundamental? It's as if all the faith invested in the educational system had been shaken. Naturally, I asked myself these same questions. After much reflection, I see two main reasons for our ignorance of this principle.

The first is our division of knowledge into distinct and often unrelated subjects. For example, we don't generally link astronomy and architecture.

The second stems from our widespread ignorance of celestial movements on the horizon, and in particular of the Sun's movement over the course of the year. In fact, few people today realize the extreme positions of the solstices, and believe that the Sun always rises in the East and sets in the West. These considerations are not at all part of everyday life in the 21st century.

If, despite everything, we put aside the idea that all this may be due to chance, we must ask ourselves what is the origin of a practice that would orientate a particular space according to the sunset on a given date.

As I've already mentioned, my own research has taken me all the way back to the very beginning of the Neolithic period, 5000 BC, and the megalithic constructions, the most important center of which is at Carnac in Brittany. Here, kilometers of upright stones arranged in alignments aim at the horizon at particular dates of sunrise and sunset to form the basis of our calendar and the division of the year into 12 months, among others.[12]

This practice was also perpetuated in Egypt, where long processional alleys obeyed the same principles. The word horizon comes from Horus-zone, the belt of Horus, the god of time. The horizon is therefore the belt of sight (the eye of Horus), but also of

---

12      Howard Crowhurst, *Carnac, The Alignments,* Epistemea, 2010

time, the belt that encircles us. The word has come into English in horology – the study and measurement of time and the art of making clocks and watches.

The orientation of churches followed exactly the same principles, for although churches are said to face due east, in reality they face towards the east and can deviate from the east-west axis by a great deal. A striking example is Chartres Cathedral, whose main axis deviates from the east-west axis by 47.05 degrees.

In their book "Introduction to the World of Symbols", Benedictine fathers Gérard de Champeaux and Sébastien Stercks[13] talk about the chrismon or Chi Rho (16).

*"The chrismon is the symbolic scheme of ritual observation of the Sun. The observer would stand in the center of the sacred place, facing east, i.e., facing the rising Sun, on a ritual seat, placed in a precise and invariable location. He followed the successive movements of heliacal rises on the horizon between the two extreme limits reached at the summer and winter solstices. These two essential points were marked on the ground by two masts or two menhirs in certain prehistoric alignments...or in more elaborate times, by two columns. Such columns have been found on both sides of some ancient temples, facing east, as was the one in Jerusalem."*

Here, two Benedictine fathers explain in no uncertain terms that the principles used in church construction date back to prehistoric times. So it's not too far-fetched to think that Louis XIII, Louis the Just, link between Heaven and Earth, wanted to orient his château according to the same principles as the Benedictine brothers.

Appendix 4, page 122, refers to Jean-François de Gondi, Archbishop of Paris, a man of Breton origin, who sold the lands of Versailles to Louis XIII. In the 17th century, he introduced into his abbey the reform of La Société de Brittany, an association of reformed Benedictine religious establishments in Brittany.

Was Louis XIII the first to notice this particular orientation of the Val de Galie? What is the origin of this relationship between the Virgin Mary and the date of August 15? What is the principle behind linking a date considered sacred to a given orientation? We'll come back to these questions later.

However, there's another very mysterious fact to add to the evidence pointing to a deep-seated intention in the orientation of Versailles towards sunset on August 15.

---

13      Gérard de Champeaux and Sebastien Stercks, *Introduction au Monde des Symboles*, éditions Zodiaque, 1991

(16) (BELOW) CHRISMON OR CHI RHO ON THE CHURCH IN COLL, CATALONIA. THIS SYMBOL INDICATES THE HORIZONTAL CARDINAL AXES IN THE CENTER AND THE TWO EXTREME AXES OF THE SOLSTICES.

(17) (ABOVE AND OPPOSITE) THE KING GOVERNS BY HIMSELF, CENTRAL PAINTING IN THE HALL OF MIRRORS, IN LINE WITH THE GRANDE PERSPECTIVE, SURMOUNTED (UPSIDE DOWN) BY "THE POMP OF FRANCE'S NEIGHBORING POWERS".

LE ROY
GOVVERNE

# THE CARD GAME CALENDAR

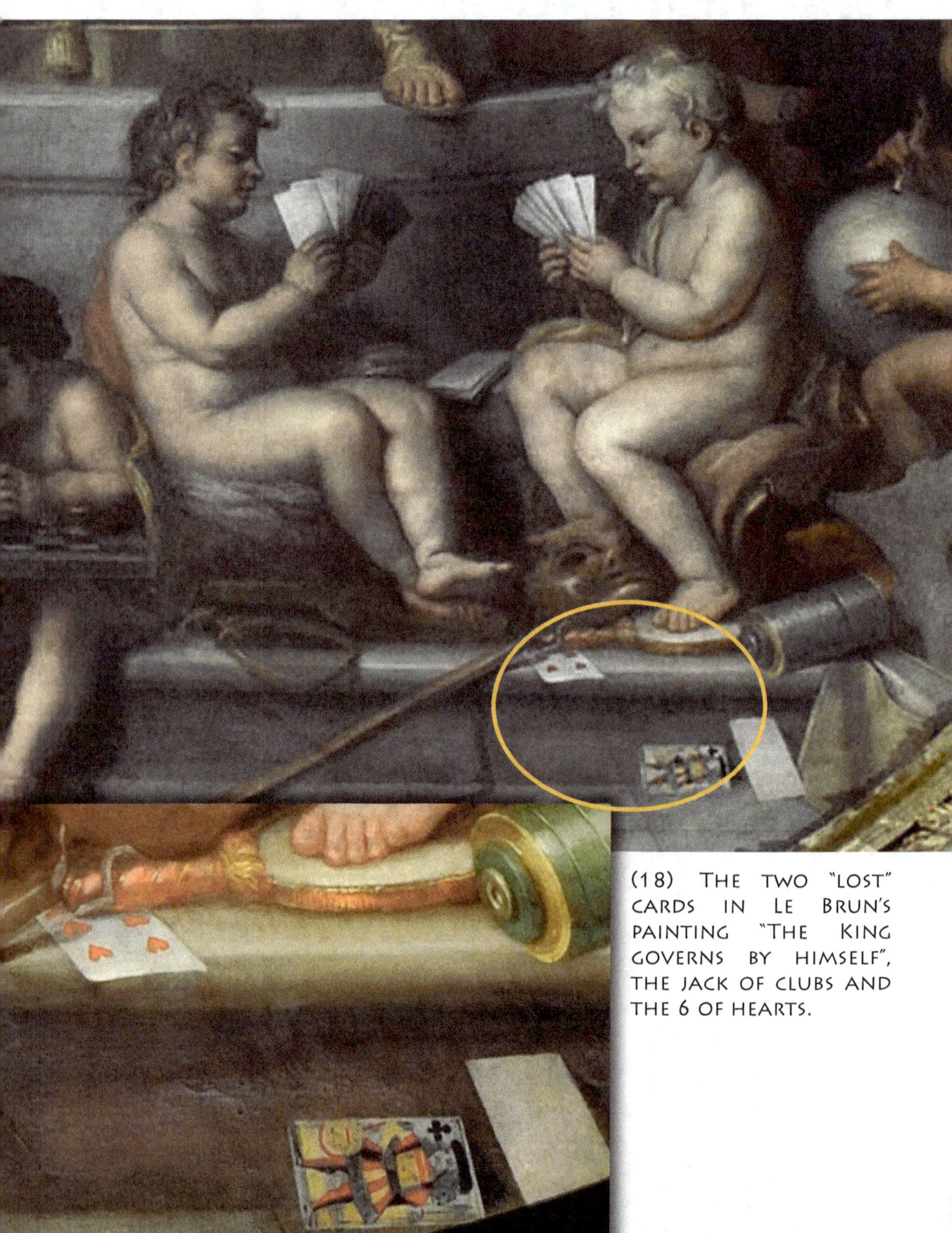

(18) THE TWO "LOST" CARDS IN LE BRUN'S PAINTING "THE KING GOVERNS BY HIMSELF", THE JACK OF CLUBS AND THE 6 OF HEARTS.

he painting "The King governs by himself"(17) , located in the center of the Hall of Mirrors and painted in 1661, "'is the main nexus of everything'" (Nivelon). We will now examine the lower part of the painting.

*All around the throne, in the foreground, the Amours represent the Genies of amusement: they write, play music, cards, checkers, amuse themselves with theatrical masks; these Genies symbolize the pleasures the king indulged in when he decided to take the reins of state into his own hands.[14]*

As I looked at it, a strange detail caught my eye. Two cards appear to have been lost by the two "Amours" playing cards. They lie on the floor and are clearly visible (18). A slightly hidden 6 of hearts is on the pedestal where the players are seated, and a perfectly visible jack of clubs is against the stair. Is it possible that these two cards were chosen "at random", or is there a hidden clue here? This was a particularly interesting question for me, as I'm the author of a book on the origins of the 52-card deck![15]

In figure (19), I've enlarged the Jack of Clubs painted by Le Brun and turned the image so that it can be seen more clearly. My research led me to discover that it corresponds to a card from the Rouen workshop, painted by Nicolas Benière and dated 1680. This drawing can be found almost identically as early as 1650 in the Rouen cards. It's interesting to see that Le Brun chose to reproduce the Rouen style, even though there were already renowned cardmakers in Paris. This shows that the Rouen school was more valued in his opinion. Although the two cards are not exactly alike, they differ little. The valet's hair, his hat, the design and color of his clothes, the orientation of his gaze: all these elements are present. There's also the medallion in the bottom right-hand corner, which was the place where the cardmaker inscribed his references. However, in Le Brun's card, the valet's chest is not divided in two by a vertical line, but features an integral yellow rectangle. We'll see the importance of this detail in a moment.

In 1893, Olney Richmond, an American author from Chicago and former world chess champion, published a book entitled "The Mystic Test Book" (20), in which he claimed that the 52-card deck had an extremely ancient origin and contained elements of a lost teaching. He relates how, after having been seriously wounded by a bullet in a Civil War battle, he was instructed in this teaching by a Frenchman who had appeared out of nowhere. Among the many revelations contained in his book, he presents a calendar

14      https://galeriedesglaces-versailles.fr/html/11/collection/c17.html
15      Howard Crowhurst, *52 mysteries, The hidden meaning of the Cards*, Epistemea, 2023.

 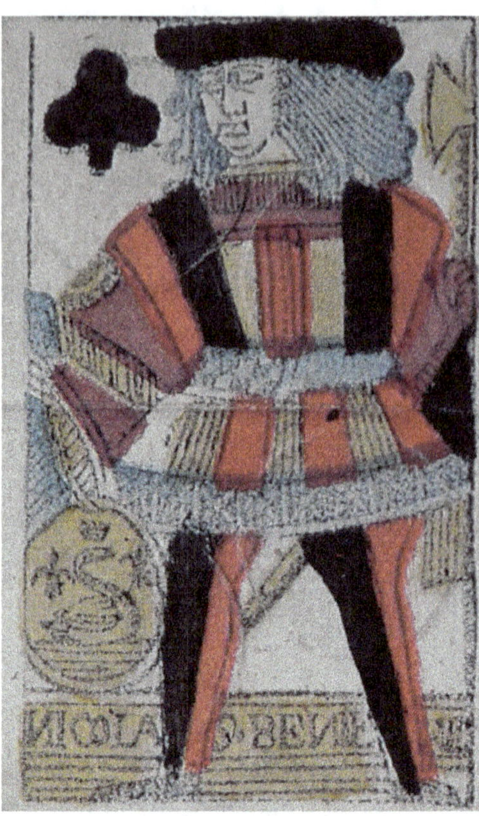

(19) (LEFT) ENLARGEMENT OF THE JACK OF CLUBS IN LE BRUN'S PAINTING WITH A SUN ON HIS CHEST.　　(RIGHT) A JACK OF CLUBS FROM THE ROUEN GAME BY NICOLAS BENIÈRE IN 1680.

(20) (LEFT) OLNEY RICHMOND'S 1893 BOOK ON THE PRINCIPLES OF A CALENDAR IN WHICH EACH DAY OF THE YEAR CORRESPONDS TO ONE OF 52 CARDS.

(21) Parisian counterfeit of a Rouen game from 1650.

where each day of the year corresponds to one of the 52 cards in the deck. Obviously, since there are 365 days in the year and only 52 cards in a deck, each card can represent several dates. However, a card can only be found once in any given zodiac sign16. The cards of the sign Leo are reinforced by the solar nature of this sign.

**In the system presented by Olney Richmond, the date of August 15, the celebration of the Virgin in the sign of Leo, corresponds to the Jack of Clubs!**

As for the 6 of hearts, it corresponds to December 25, the birth date of Christ, the solar hero born of the Virgin. When this date was fixed by the Church in the 4th century, it corresponded to the winter solstice in the Julian calendar. The name Noel comes from "Novo Helios", the new Sun. The solar nature of Christ is also indicated by the age given to him at the time of his crucifixion, 33 years[17].

This information, though real, could be mistaken for coincidence, because if it isn't, what does it mean?

Another fact, however, points to a proven intention behind the presence of these cards.

*In 1701, Louis XIV imposed a tax on card games and redesigned the portrait. The compulsory marks were three fleurs-de-lys in a circle and the words "G. DE PARIS" (Généralité de Paris). The breastplate of the Jack of Clubs shows a sun[18].*

16    Ibid. The principles of this calendar are explained on pages 109-110.

17    33 years is a cycle that combines astronomical day and year lengths, since 365.2422 days, the exact length of a solar year, multiplied by 33 gives 12052.9926 days, a deviation of less than 11 minutes from a whole number of days. The leap years every 4 years in our calendar leave a gap of 45 minutes with the astronomical cycles. In 32 years, i.e. 8 leap cycles, the difference is 8 times 45 minutes, or 6 hours. The 33-year cycle is therefore much more precise.

18    http://christian.deryck.free.fr/Valet/Paris/index.htm

Louis XIV, King of France and Navarre, intervened to impose the design of a sun on the chest of the Jack of Clubs! From 1701 until 1717, two years after his death, all representations of the Jack of Clubs produced by French cardmakers had to feature a Sun (22).

Was this rule already applied by Le Brun as early as 1661?

(22) (LEFT) NICOLAS LEROY'S JACK OF CLUBS, 1710. (RIGHT) A JACK OF CLUBS
FROM THE P. PELLÉ SET, 1710. (BELOW) AN 18TH-CENTURY CARD FROM THE
COLLECTION OF PHILIPPE PICOT DE LAPEYROUSE IN TOULOUSE. THE DIRECTION
OF THE LOOK AND THE POSITION OF THE CLUB ARE REVERSED.

# THE SACRED NATURE OF THE LATITUDE OF VERSAILLES



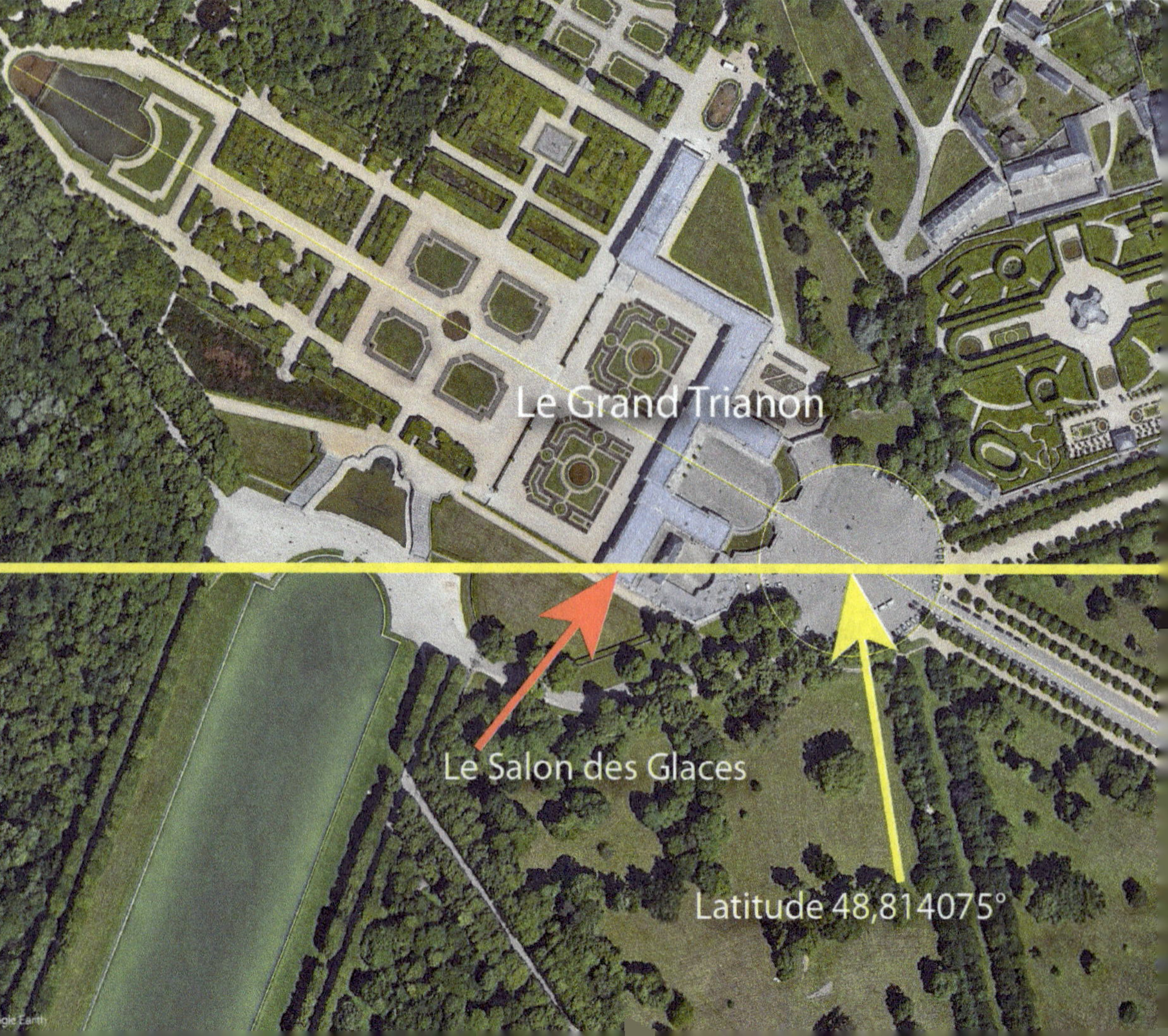

**A**t Versailles, Louis XIV didn't just embellish and enlarge his father's work. From 1670, at the age of 32, he had a second château built to the northwest of the first, the Château du Trianon.

*"I made Versailles for my Court, Marly for my friends and Trianon for myself" - Louis XIV.*

We'll come back to the details of this magnificent building's layout and integration into the overall plan later. For now, it's the location that concerns us[19].

In the center of the circle at the entrance to the Château du Trianon in Versailles, at latitude 48.814075°N,

**a 7-meter-high mast would cast a shadow exactly 8 meters long**

at solar noon on the day of the equinox[20].

This fact is quite remarkable, and we'll see in Volume 2 that this relationship between seven and eight is clearly represented in the Colonnade grove. The probability of this

---

19      For a better understanding of what is to follow, consult "Appendix 2. Equinoxes and latitudes.", page 115

20      $\text{Tan}(48{,}814075°) = 1{,}142857 = 8/7$

(24) SACRED LATITUDE 8/7 OF THE GRAND TRIANON (ZOOM).

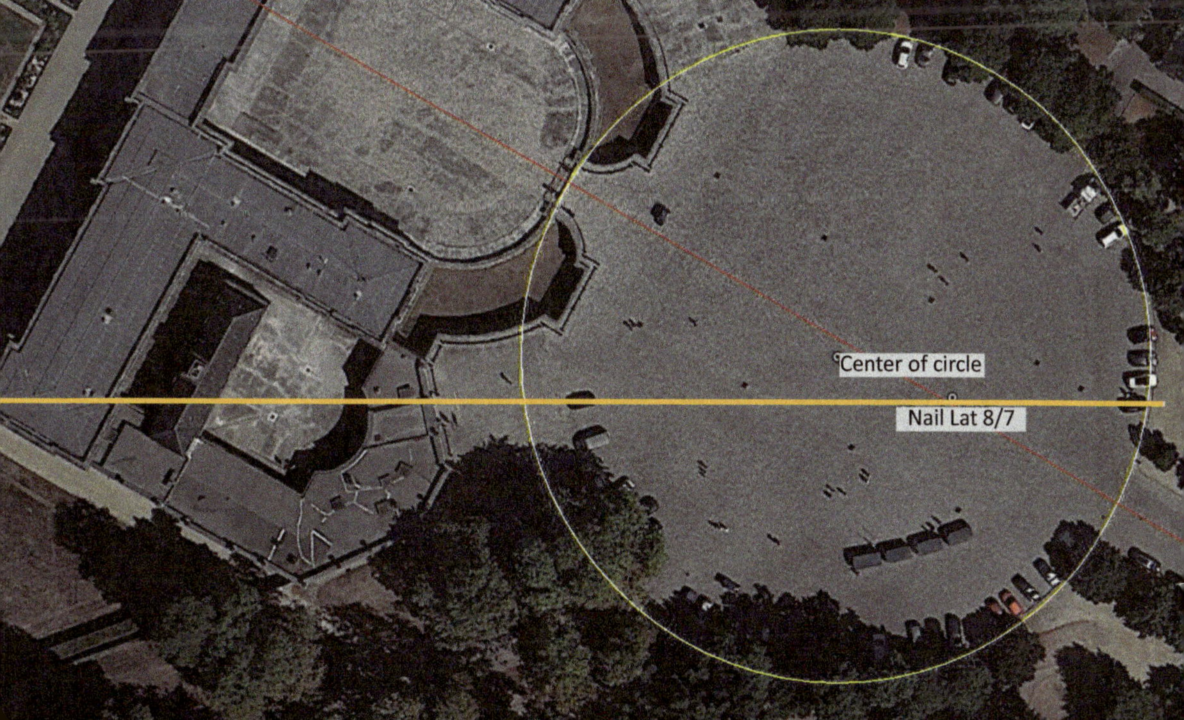

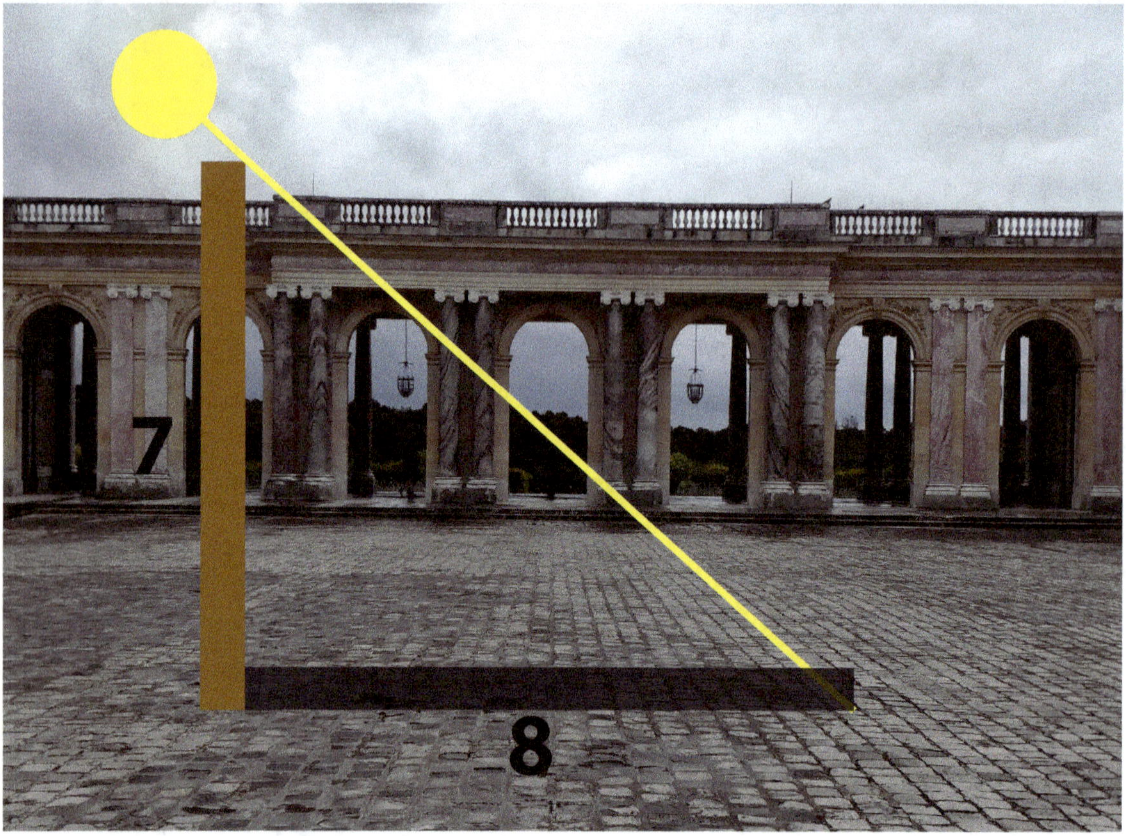

(25) The ratio between the height of a pillar and the length of its shadow at noon on the equinox at the latitude of the Grand Trianon (48.814075° or 48°48.845') is 7 to 8, or 1/1.142857.

(26) The nail marking latitude 8/7 in the axis of the Château du Trianon.

fact being due to chance is very close to zero, and we must consider it as one of the reasons why Louis XIV decided to settle here.

You'd have to travel more than 65 kilometers north to find a latitude with similar characteristics, a ratio of 6 to 7 between a mast and its shadow, or 50 kilometers south, a ratio of 8 to 9. I haven't found any buildings of note at these latitudes in France.

This latitude passes through the northern limit of the Grand Canal and also through the Salon of Mirrors (28) in the Château du Trianon. This is the southernmost room in the château, overlooking the Grand Canal to the west, and was Louis XIV's ancient study. It was here that he gathered the members of his council. The walls and doors of this salon are lined with mirrors, just like the Hall of Mirrors at the Château de Versailles.

Although there are currently no pillars or masts on the premises at Versailles, a small detail may well reveal the reality of this intention. When I told a friend about this strange feature of the Trianon's latitude, he went to the site and began scrutinizing the cobblestones that make up the floor of the vast circular courtyard in front of the Château's entrance gates. It was there, with great emotion, that he discovered a nail embedded in a paving stone in the axis of the Trianon and its driveway. This nail is at the exact latitude of 8/7 (26) and (27).

I haven't been able to find the slightest clue as to the reason for this nail's existence, which goes completely unnoticed by the thousands of people who visit the site every day. However, it is quite possible that it is a reference point for a surveyor's layout.

(27) THE NAIL IN THE CENTER OF THE TRIANON AND ITS AVENUE.

(28) The Salon of mirrors at the Grand Trianon.

(29) The seven arches of the Trianon Peristyle.

For anyone studying the principles of placing sacred sites, the example of the Trianon's latitude shows an obvious intention, all the more so as the relationship generated, 1 + 1/7 or 1 + 0.142857 (25), is an indication of the presence of Ancient Science. The division of the unit into seven parts was a well-known principle in ancient Egypt. The cubit was divided into seven palms. The angles of the pyramid slopes (seked) were determined according to this division by seven. We still have remnants of these principles in our daily lives, with the division of the week into 7 days and the division of the musical octave into 7 whole tones.

Between the northern and southern parts of the Château du Trianon lies a construction called "the Peristyle" by Louis XIV himself, although the name Loggia would better reflect the architecture of the building.

*He is also the creator of the Peristyle, although the design of the arcade is by Robert de Cotte, the idea of the central breakthrough that provides a view of the garden is by Louis XIV. The arcades were intended to be closed by woodwork, but the decision not to install it was taken while Mansart was out taking the waters. In keeping with tradition, the quality of the stone used was adapted to the nature of the area being treated, but Louis XIV imposed the use of a single quality of stone to ensure unity of color.[21].*

The transparency of this construction is fundamental to the King's project, and we'll come back to this later. For now, let's just note that the Peristyle is made up of seven vaults and eight sets of two columns (29).

As we shall see, while the latitude of the Grand Trianon, the King's residence, is perfectly in keeping with an unusual destiny, the orientation chosen for the château and its avenues will reveal other considerations. Let's continue our examination of solar movement on the horizon[22] and its role in determining an ancient calendar, once widespread but now forgotten.

---

21      Mathieu da Vinha and Raphaël Masson, *Versailles pour les nuls*, First & Château de Versailles, mars 2011

22      See "Appendix 3. Solstices", page 118

# The Celtic calendar at Versailles

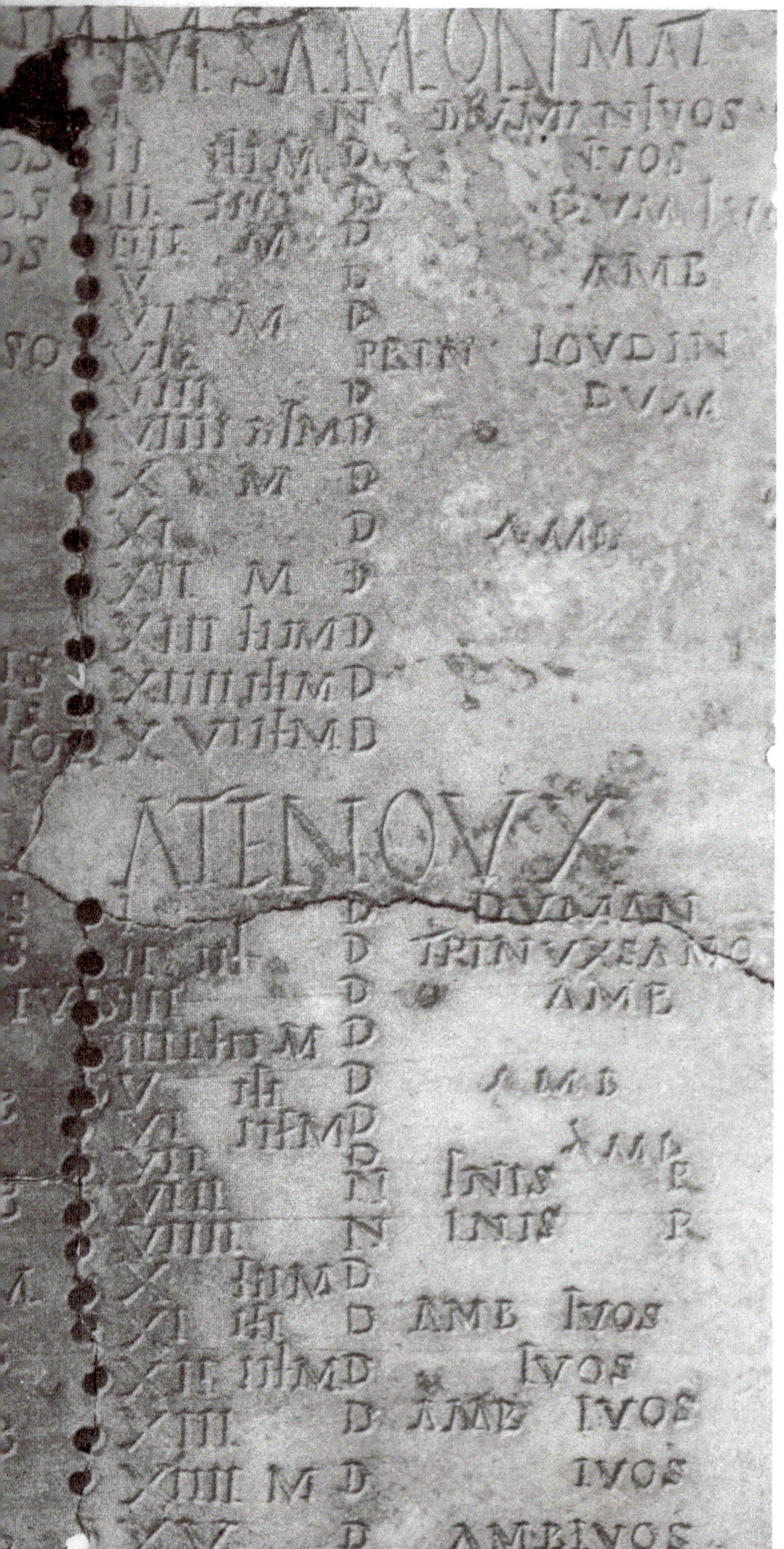

(30) A reconstructed piece of the Coligny calendar. The holes were used to place a pawn to mark the date.

efore the Roman invasion, the Gauls used a highly complex calendar that followed both the positions of the sun and the moon over a five-year period, called a lustre. We know some of the details of this calendar, but not everything, thanks to bronze fragments discovered at Coligny in the Ain region of France in 1897, with notations written in the Gallic language (30). Without going into all the details of this calendar, for the purposes of this book we'll look at the four major solar festivals that punctuate it and have left their mark on the current calendar in France[23].

These four festivals are:

**November 1**, the festival of the Druids, called Samhain, the beginning of the Celtic year, now known as the Day of the Dead, a public holiday in France.

**February 1**, the festival of craftsmen, called Imbolc, often confused with Saint Brigid's Day.

**May 1**, the festival of warriors and Bel, the sun god, called Beltane, now known as Labor Day, a public holiday in France.

**August 1**, the festival of the king, bringing together the three castes[24], called Lugnasad, today the Swiss national holiday.

Each of these festivals takes place 40 days after the beginning of a season.

The feast began at sunset the day before. Two of these festivals still exist today:

**Halloween** on October 31, the eve of the Day of the Dead, and

**Walpurgisnacht**, still very popular in the Nordic countries, which takes place on the evening of April 30.

Compared with the four dates of the solstices and equinoxes[25], this calendar divides the seasons asymmetrically. (32) The average 91 days in a season are divided with 40 days on one side and 51 days on the other. This fact is very important from the point of view of observing the sunrise and sunset axes during these Celtic festivals.

Whereas the axis of sunset at the winter solstice corresponds to the same axis as sunrise at the summer solstice, but seen in the other direction, as we have seen, the

---

23      For more details, consult the reference book on the subject, Françoise Le Roux and Christian-J. Guyonvarc'h, *Les Fêtes Celtiques,* Editions Yoran, Fouesnant, 2015

24      The three castes of society were druids, warriors and craftsmen.

25      see "Appendix 1. Equinoxes and cardinal axes.", page 112 and "Appendix 3. Solstices", page 118.

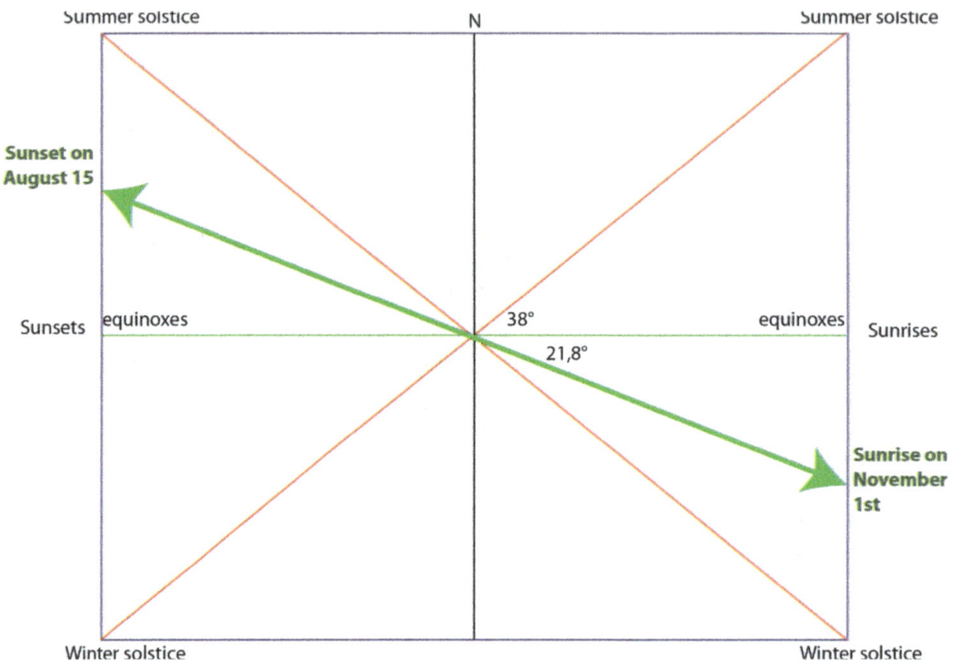


(31) The axis of sunrise on November 1st corresponds to the axis of sunset on August 15th. This is the axis of the Grande Perspective of Versailles.

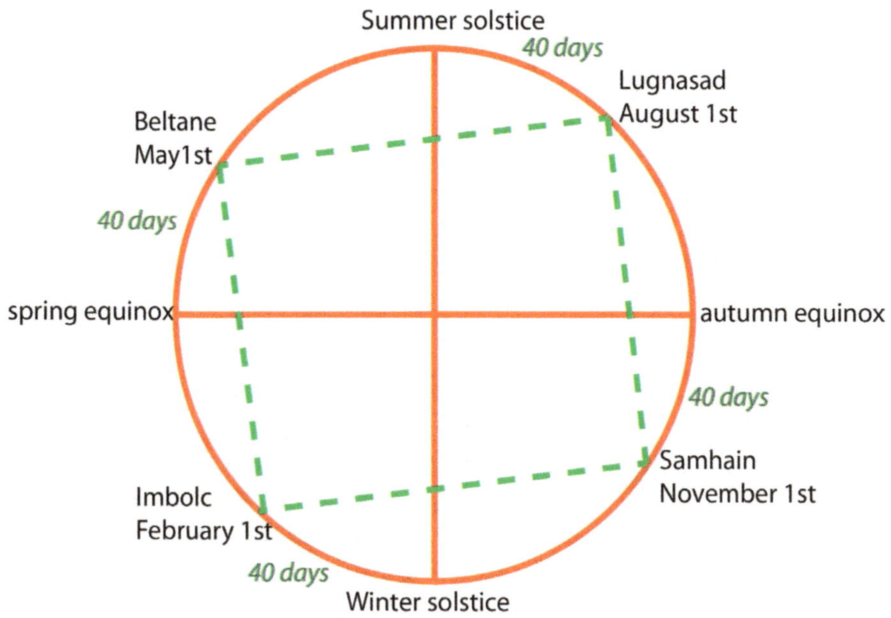


(32) THE CELTIC CALENDAR, WITH ITS FOUR MAJOR FESTIVALS 40 DAYS AFTER THE START OF EACH SEASON.

axis of sunrise on November 1 corresponds to sunset on August 15. (31)

Obviously, given what we've seen of the main axis of the Château de Versailles, known as La Grande Perspective, this fact is of the utmost importance, as we discover that this axis also corresponds to the sunrise of the most important festival in the ancient Gallic calendar, as it marked the beginning of the year. The King could watch this sunrise from his bedroom (33).

## THE ORIGIN OF OUR CALENDAR

The 40-day period expressed in the Celtic calendar echoes the same period expressed in the Hebrew Bible or Old Testament. In Genesis, we are told the story of the flood and Noah's ark. It rained for 40 days and 40 nights. In the New Testament of the Christian Bible, Mary returned to the Temple 40 days after giving birth (on the winter solstice[26]),

26      Wikipedia, *Christmas*, "In the early fourth century, the church fixed the date of Christmas on December 25. This corresponded to the traditional date of the winter solstice in the Roman calendar. It is exactly nine months after Annunciation on March 25, also the date of

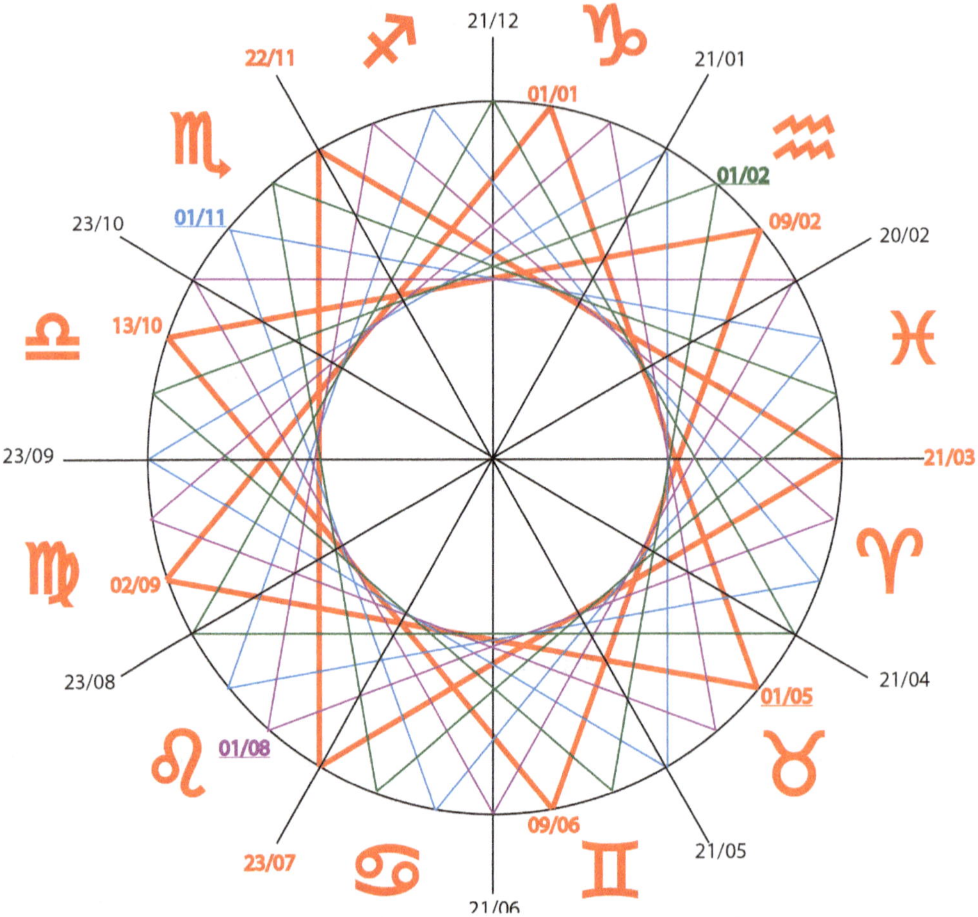

21/12
22/11
21/01
01/01
23/10
01/11
01/02
09/02
20/02
13/10
21/03
23/09
02/09
23/08
21/04
01/05
01/08
21/05
23/07
09/06
21/06

and Christ stayed in the desert for 40 days.

These texts therefore refer to a period of 40 days, known in our time as quarantine, which implies the division of the year into 9 months of 40 days, making a total of 360 days. To this we add five days, known in Egypt as epagomena, or public holidays, which are outside the calendar. These additional days were mainly inserted into the calendar in spring and summer, as these seasons last 93 days compared to autumn and winter, which last only 89-90 days.

Until 50 BC, the Roman year began on the vernal equinox. It was Julius Caesar who set January 1 as the start of the year.

**The January 1 date that marks the beginning of our calendar is exactly 80 days before the vernal equinox. This would be the start of the 7th month of 40 days.**

As a result of Julius Caesar's modification, all the Celtic feasts are positioned on the first of the month, giving them an importance in today's calendar as moments of new energy.

It's interesting to note that two of these great Celtic festivals, May 1st and November 1st, are still celebrated as public holidays in France. As for August 1st, it is honored in Switzerland, as it is the date of the national feast day. The date opposite November 1, August 15, is also a public holiday in France. As for the other French public holidays, 3 of them are linked to Easter (Easter Monday, Ascension Thursday, 40 days after Easter, and Pentecost Monday, 11 days later), which is itself linked to the Spring equinox. November 11, which commemorates the Armistice of the First World war, is exactly 40 days before the winter solstice on December 21.

Why did Caesar move the start of the year to January 1? Could it have been influenced by his encounter with druids during his invasion of Gaul? Or was it a way of facilitating acceptance of Roman occupation by Gaulish leaders, and thus laying the foundations for over four centuries of collaboration?

Let's return to our main subject, the layout of the different axes at Versailles.

---

the spring equinox." Winter solstice became the 21st December in the 16th century after the change to the Gregorian calendar.

(33) (Opposite) Sunrise on November 1, 2022 from the King's bedroom in the Château of Louis XIII. The photograph shows how the axis is flat over a long distance, enabling very precise aiming.

# Louis XIV and the axis of the Château du Trianon

(34) Image from www.SunCalc.net for August 1st at Versailles. Sunrise is the yellow line, sunset is the orange line.

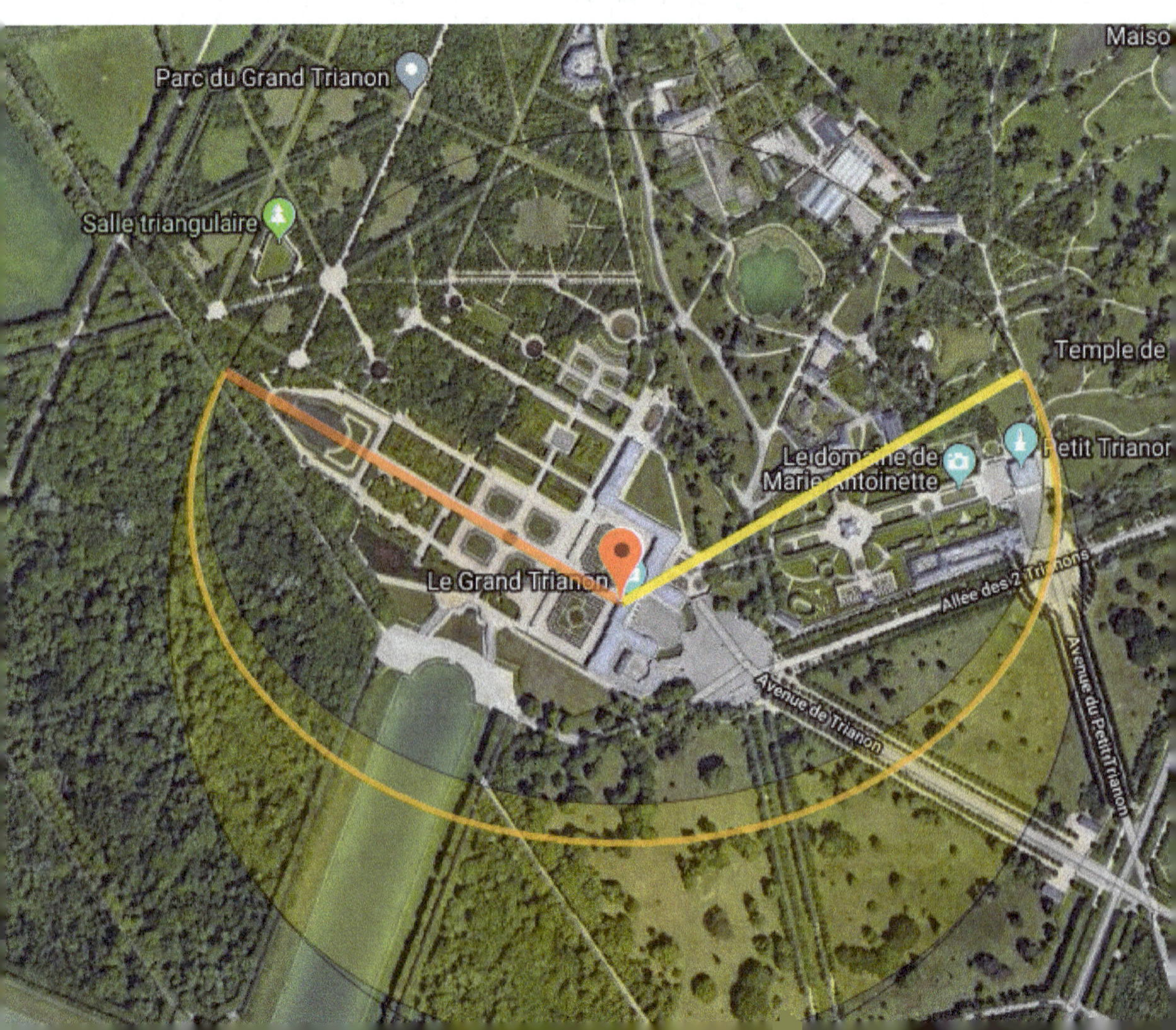

A cursory examination of the layout of the Versailles estate in Louis XIV's time reveals another axis, the one that starts at the Dragon Fountain near the Neptune Fountain and leads to the center of the Peristyle of the Château du Grand Trianon, which Louis XIV claims to have built for himself.

It was the king himself who supervised the work, installed in a tent nearby. He was attentive to the smallest details, and had walls knocked down that he felt did not conform to his vision. As we have already mentioned, the idea of the Peristyle, the central opening that allows views to both sides along the axis through the château, was conceived by Louis XIV himself.

This axis is slightly offset to the north in relation to the Grande Perspective, with an angle of 29.25° from the east-west axis, i.e. 7.45° north of the château's main axis, which is 21.8°. The two axes meet in the Dragon Fountain, whose center is on the axis of the Water Walk and the Lake of the Swiss Guard, perpendicular to the Grande Perspective (see plan on inside cover).

Now, the axis of the Trianon (34) corresponds to

**the axis of sunset on August 1st (40), the king's feast day in the Celtic calendar.**

According to Wikipedia for Lugnasad (the August 1st festival):

*This is the feast of the king in his role as redistributor of wealth and fairness, under the authority of the druids. It's a military truce celebrating peace, friendship, abundance and prosperity for the kingdom. It is compulsory and brings together the three classes (priestly, warrior and craftsmen) of Celtic society..*

(35) THE TWO AXES OF VERSAILLES MEET AT THE DRAGON FOUNTAIN.

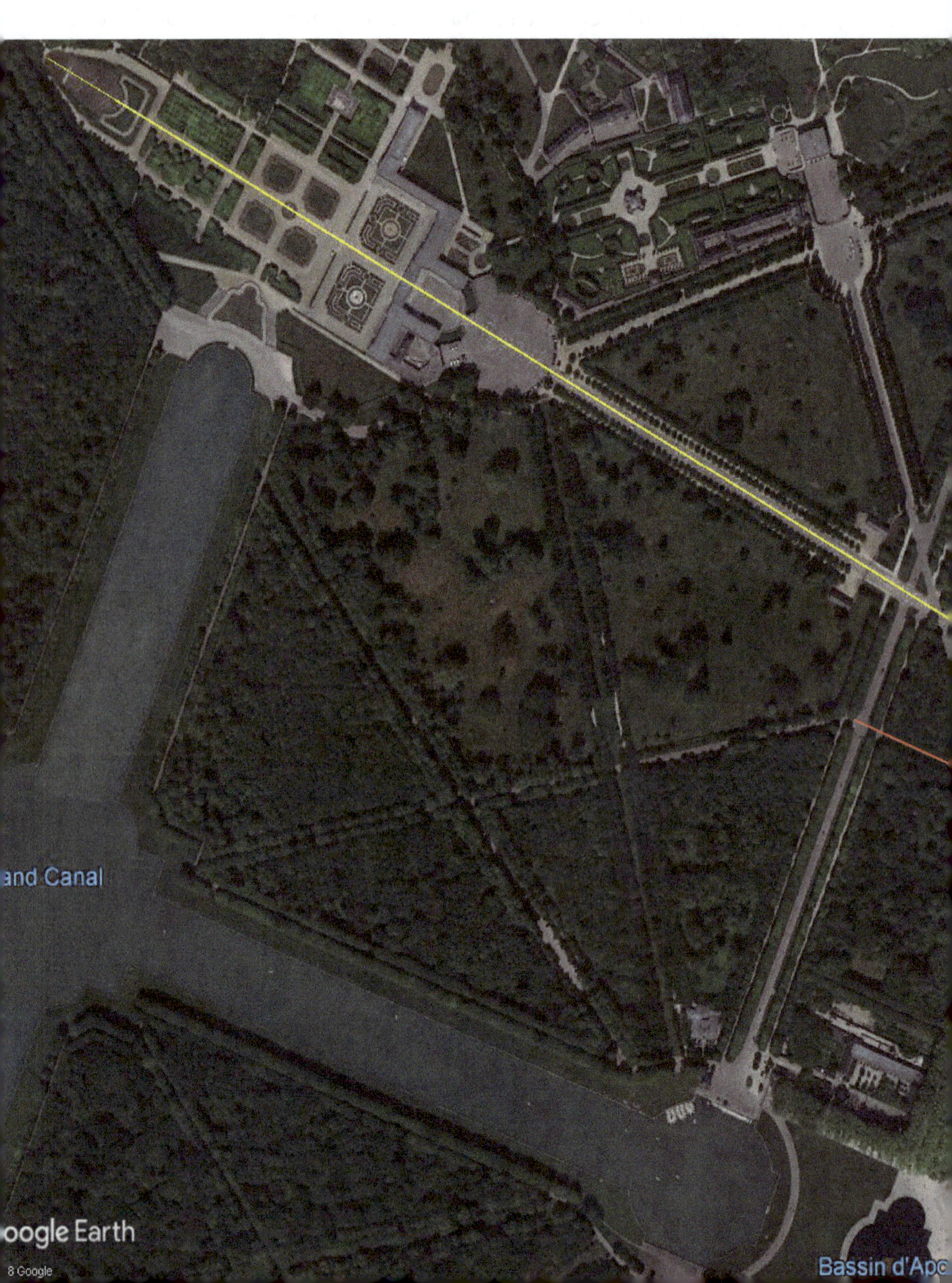
and Canal
oogle Earth
8 Google
Bassin d'Apo

(36) The Trianon axis (in yellow) runs from the Dragon Fountain through the château and gardens at an angle of 299.25° from the north, or 29.25° north-west. The main axis (the Grande Perspective) is marked in red. The center of the Dragon Fountain is exactly 700m east of the center of the Enceladus grove. This line (in green) also passes through the center of the Flora fountain.


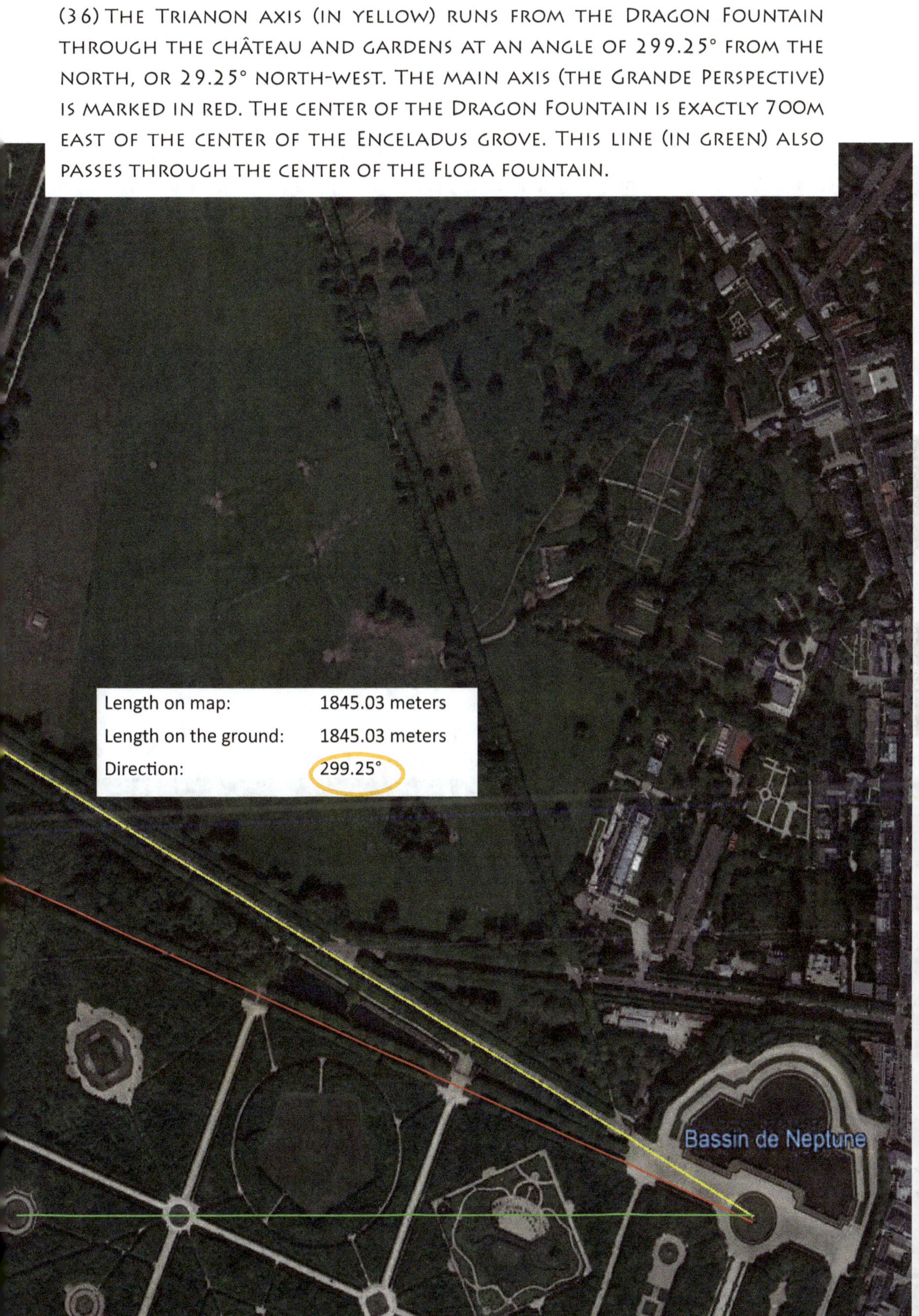

Length on map:          1845.03 meters
Length on the ground:   1845.03 meters
Direction:              299.25°
Bassin de Neptune

**We thus discover that the two major axes of Versailles correspond to the solar axis of two major Celtic festivals, November 1 and August 1. What's more, the axis of sunrise on November 1st corresponds in the opposite direction to the axis of sunset on August 15th.**

In the Dragon Fountain, which joins the two axes, the main axis passes through the dragon's head (12), while the Trianon axis passes through its tail (35). Again, this simple fact cannot be insignificant. August 1st and August 15th are both in the astrological sign of Leo, the solar fire sign. They are united by the body of the dragon, whose igneous aspect is obvious. The main star of the Leo constellation is Regulus, the King's Star.

In the overall layout of the gardens, the adjustment between these two axes can be seen in the irregular shape of the small copses and water features to the north of the main copses (37). The same offset is mirrored on the south side of the southern groves.

In a previous book, I was able to show[27] that these orientations were of great importance to the megalith builders at Carnac in Brittany. A stone rectangle at a place called Le Manio in Carnac shows exactly these two axes of August 1st and November 1st, but oriented towards the rising of August 1st and the setting of November 1st (38). Its two non-parallel sides are identical, but inverted, to the irregular shape of the Versailles groves.

---

27  *La Science des Anciens, tome 2, Carnac, Le Manio,* éditions Epistemea, 2015

(38) THE MEGALITHIC QUADRILATERAL OF LE MANIO IN CARNAC, DATING FROM AROUND 4000 BC, WITH ITS TWO NON-PARALLEL SIDES ORIENTED TOWARDS THE AUGUST 1ST SUNRISE (IN RED) AND THE NOVEMBER 1ST SUNSET (IN YELLOW), DEMONSTRATING THE NON-SYMMETRICAL ASPECT OF THE CELTIC CALENDAR.

(39) THE SAME QUADRILATERAL AT THE LATITUDE OF VERSAILLES.

At Versailles, therefore, the Sun sets in line with the Trianon on August 1st. Two weeks later, on August 15, when the Sun has moved a little further south and the days are a little shorter, it sets in the axis of the Grand Perspective. Now, another astonishing fact adds to the mystery. In Orthodox Christianity, as practiced by the Copts in Egypt (see below), between August 1 and August 15, there is a period of fasting called the Dormition Fast.

*This two-week Lenten period combines three dimensions. On August 1, the Holy and life-giving Cross is remembered, water is blessed, and a procession with the Cross is held, as was done in Constantinople in the past. And so begins a **40-day period** that will conclude with the Veneration of September 14th. During this glorious fortnight, the usual abstinence (wine, oil, animal products) is observed, except on the 6th*[28].

**So August 1 in the Orthodox calendar begins a period of 40 days, exactly as in the Celtic calendar.**

What's more, the period between August 1 and August 15 is marked by Lent, a 15-day fasting period.

Could it be that the origin of the feast of the Virgin Mary on August 15 is much more ancient than the Virgin Mary herself?

28      https://sagesse-orthodoxe.fr/jaimerais-savoir/foi-et-tradition-orthodoxe/foi-de-leglise/le-jeune-de-la-dormition

This question leads us to another mystery that concerns Versailles: that of the marshes. For if, as we mentioned at the outset, the château's location seemed inappropriate to court observers because of the violent winds that regularly swept across the summit, the land was also notoriously unhealthy. The work achieved to clean up the marshes was phenomenal, with the creation of huge fountains such as the Lake of the Swiss Guard and the Grand Canal.

However, this type of work was not new to the region. The city of Paris had initially been built by draining the marshes on either side of the Île de la Cité.

Indeed, the ancient name of Paris, Lutetia, is thought to have meant "marsh".

This francization of Lutetia comes from the Gallic radical lut- "marsh", to be compared with the Gaelic loth "marsh" and Breton loudour "unclean"»[29].

Fascination with marshlands goes back a long way in human history. Isis, the most famous goddess of ancient Egypt, herself lived in the marshlands, and the temples built

---

29      Albert Deshayes, *Dictionnaire étymologique du breton*, Douarnenez, Le Chasse-Marée, 2003, p. 472, 475

(40) SUNSET ON JULY 31, 2020 IN THE AXIS OF THE TRIANON. WITH THE HORIZON BLOCKED BY VEGETATION, A YELLOW LINE SHOWS THE SUN'S PATH TOWARDS THE CENTER OF THE PERISTYLE.

in her honor were mostly on mounds surrounded by swamps.

Now, the main festivals celebrated in honor of Isis in Egypt were agricultural ones, such as the "Harvest Festival", for which the Egyptians reserved the first ears of wheat for this goddess considered, along with her husband Osiris, to be the inventor of wheat. It's this relationship that is shown on drawings of the Virgin in representations of the zodiac, where she holds an ear of corn. It's also the origin of the name of the star Spica (spike), the brightest star in the Virgo constellation.

But where does the August 15 date for celebrating Virgo come from, given that the zodiacal sign of Virgo begins on August 23, eight days later?

# Where does the August 15 celebration come from?

(41) Representation of Saint Mark with a horse's head from Lande-vennec Abbey in Britanny. "Marc'h" in Breton means horse.

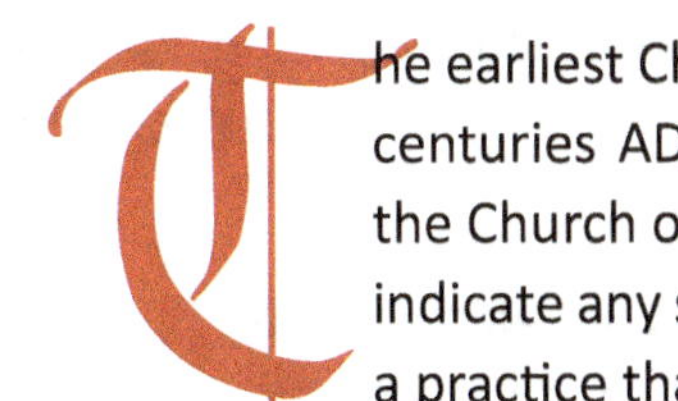he earliest Christian celebrations of August 15 date back to the first centuries AD, when torch-lit night processions were practiced by the Church of Rome. Why this date? There's nothing in the Bible to indicate any such activity at this time of year. And why a procession, a practice that probably originated in Egypt?

*Since the Ptolemies, pharaohs of Greek origin, Egyptians have been known as Copts. Evangelized by Saint Mark, Alexandria became Christian in 42 AD. Today, Egyptian Christians, authentic descendants of Pharaonic Egypt in culture, are called Copts. The Copts of Egypt have a special veneration for the Virgin Mary, whose Assumption is celebrated throughout the Christian world on August 15[30].*

It is estimated that in the 5th century, only 10% of Europeans were Christians, which means that 90% believed something else. The idea of eliminating heresies eventually led to the Inquisition, which didn't appear until 600 years later. The stronghold of early Christianity was in Egypt and Ethiopia, where between 20% and 30% of the population followed the Christian faith. The practice of monastic life and hermitage, common to all Breton saints, was first recorded among the Coptic desert monks, who re-enacted Jesus' 40-day fast in the desert. A sophisticated calendar of feast days already existed, whose origins were to be found in Egyptian and Babylonian sources. There are striking similarities between certain Coptic practices and those of the first Breton monks at Landévennec Abbey, where the monks settled as early as the 7th century. They produced evangeliaries, books that are above all religious works (41).

*The monks didn't just write, they illustrated the texts. Under their pen, the evangelists became strange creatures - "zoo-anthropomorphic" beings, as specialists call them - with a human body and the head of their animal symbol. This practice is common to the Copts of Egypt and the island monasteries of Ireland and Great Britain[31].*

Could there be traces of contact between these early monks of Brittany, who set up their hermitages in the forest like the Druids, and the Copts of Egypt? It's not unreason-

---

30      http://eocf.free.fr/print_press_revest_15_aout.htm

31      *Landévennec, haut lieu de la spiritualité bretonne*, Erwan Chartier-Le Floch, Histoire de Bretagne, 25 Juillet 2010

able to think that practitioners of the ancient Celtic religion used the nascent Christianity to spread their own beliefs.[32]

In the 6th century, the Byzantine emperor Maurice introduced the feast days of the Dormition of the Virgin Mary on August 15, apparently to commemorate the inauguration of a church dedicated to the Virgin Mary, the Sepulchre of Mary.

The feast was introduced to Western Europe under the influence of Pope Theodore in the 7th century, and from the following century took the name of Assumption, which is not quite the same thing. In 813, the Council of Mainz listed it as one of the obligatory feast days.

However, the beginning of the sign of Virgo is August 23, not August 15, the day on which it is celebrated. Where does this discrepancy come from? A closer look at history reveals that August 15 was the first day of the octave of the Virgin, an entire week during which prayers were focused on her, a practice that disappeared in 1955.

The octave of the Assumption of St. Mary, between August 15 and 22 inclusive, was instituted by Pope Leo IV (847-855). This octave linked the ancient Druidic feast days of the Virgin, based on the orientation of the setting sun on August 15 opposite the rising sun on November 1, with the 12-month zodiacal calendar based on 30-day periods. The octave of the Assumption of the Virgin, her ascent to Heaven, thus indicates the passage from her solar nature on August 15 to her stellar nature, the constellation of Virgo. We'll see later that the date August 15 is also of interest in the way it divides the season.

---

32      For more on this subject, see my book *The Megalithic Plan*, Epistemea, 2022

(42) OPPOSITE) AT 4.30PM ON AUGUST 23RD EVERY YEAR AT CHARTRES CATHEDRAL, THE SUN IS EXACTLY ON THE AXIS THAT CONNECTS THE CENTER OF THE WEST ROSE WINDOW TO THE CENTER OF THE LABYRINTH. THESE TWO CIRCLES, WHICH ARE EXACTLY THE SAME SIZE, ARE CONNECTED BY AN ANGLE OF EXACTLY 45°. THE HEIGHT OF THE CENTER OF THE ROSE WINDOW IS IDENTICAL TO THE DISTANCE BETWEEN THE ENTRANCE AND THE CENTER OF THE LABYRINTH. UNFORTUNATELY, A TREATMENT APPLIED TO THE STAINED GLASS WINDOWS TO PROTECT THEM IN 2018 DIFFUSES THE LIGHT, PREVENTING THE RAYS FROM ILLUMINATING THE LABYRINTH AS THEY ONCE DID. IN CHARTRES, ASTRO-GEOMETRY WAS ALREADY BEING PRACTICED IN THE EARLY 13TH CENTURY.

# The Saints and Godesses of the Marshes

(43) The annual procession of Sainte-Anne-Le-Palud in Plonévez-Porzay, Brittany. Saint Anne holds an open book and teaches a child.

aint Anne-la-Palud, mother of Mary, is an important figure in Breton legend. Since "palud" means "swamp or marsh" in Old French (palus in Latin), there's a possible link with the Irish mother goddess "De Ana", goddess of fertility, but also goddess of death who ruled over the marshes. The disease known as paludism or malaria, often contracted in marshy areas and which led to the death of thousands of people during the construction of Versailles, is therefore linked to Saint Anne-la-Palud. Another strong link can be made with the Egyptian goddess Isis, who lived in the marshlands. We'll come back to this later. The installation of the Versailles estate on a site surrounded by marshes would reinforce a possible link with these characters.

The chapel of Sainte-Anne-la-Palud in Plonévez-Porzay, Finistère, Brittany is the site of an extremely ancient and well-attended procession that used to last several days around the last Sunday in August, at harvest time. This date falls at the beginning of the astrological sign of Virgo. The pre-Christian origins of this procession are obvious to all who have taken part.

*«When the procession unfolds its ancestral phantasmagoria of costumes, banners and flickering candles, it's not hard to drift back to the fantasies when, under the Druidic oaks, Viviane, as yet still possessed, led the men of King Gradlon and Conan Mériadec to the ponds of perdition. »[33]*

According to tradition, the Sainte-Anne-la-Palud pilgrimage was established around the year 500 by Saint Corentin and Saint Guénolé de Landévennec on land at the head of Douarnenez Bay, given to Saint Anne by King Gradlon after the town of Ys was submerged. The chapel would later be submerged in its turn. The construction of the town of Ys in a flood zone, followed by the construction of a chapel, is a reminder of the need to create sacred places in the middle of marshes. Could there be a link between the town of Ys and Isis?

There's still an ancient path leading to the vanished chapel on the beach, called in Breton Hent Santez Anna Gollet (the path of Saint Anne the Vanished).

Little is known about the life of Saint Anne-la-Palud. Here's what Gustave Geffroy had to say in 1903:

---

33      Laurent Tailhade, *Santez Anna ar Palud*, Plâtres et marbres, Athéna, Paris, 6e édition, 1922 . Text written in 1903.

*« Married to a mean and jealous lord who hated children and didn't want to have any, Anne was mistreated and chased away one night by her husband, the moment he realized she was about to give birth. The poor woman abandoned the château de Moëllien and headed for the sea, where she saw a glimmer of light. It came from a boat steered by an angel. She climbed aboard, sailed for a long, long time, and finally landed in Judea, where she gave birth to the Virgin Mary. She returned to Armorica (Brittany) in the same way, where she was greeted with great joy, for she was believed to have the power to calm the elements and heal illnesses. Years and years after her return, she was visited by her grandson, Jesus, who came to ask for her blessing before beginning to preach the Gospel. At his grandmother's request, Jesus created a fountain, and the chapel was built next to it as a refuge for the sick and destitute. When Anne died, people searched everywhere in vain for her remains, which were not found until many years later, encrusted with shells, floating in the sea. »*

Anne, Mary's mother, would therefore be of Breton origin! What's more, she returned home, leaving her daughter in Judea. We can assume that the angel who accompanied her on this long journey explained to her the fate of her daughter, who would later give birth.

*On September 20, 1996, Pope John Paul II made a pilgrimage to the town of Sainte-Anne d'Auray in Brittany, bringing together 150,000 people. It was the first papal visit to Brittany. The town's Breton name is Santez Anna Wened (Sainte-Anne-La Blanche). In the past, it was known as Ker Anna, which in Breton means Anne's village. According to an oral tradition spread by the region's Christian faithful, Ker Anna was named after Saint Anne, but this toponymy is the result of a syncretism between the old pagan background of the goddess Dana and the cult of Christian saints[34].*

The name of the Irish goddess De Ana probably derives from the Indo-European root ana, meaning "breath, soul", which gave rise to the Latin word anima, taken up by Jung to represent the feminine in the human imagination. It would therefore be an archetype in the collective unconscious, enabling it to cross countries and centuries.

---

34    Frañses Favereau, *Bretagne contemporaine : langue, culture, identité*, Skol Vreizh, 1993, p. 110

# Virgo Pariturae and the druids of Chartres

The story of Saint Anne takes us right into one of the mysterious aspects of ancient Druidism: the idea of virgo parituræ, the virgin who must give birth.

This name, inscribed on the base of the black Madonna Notre-Dame-sous-Terre in the crypt of Chartres Cathedral, is said to have come from the Carnute Druids, a people of Celtic Gaul who farmed the rich Beauce plateau and are mentioned by Julius Caesar. According to legend, these druids knew that the new Messiah would be born of a virgin, and they awaited the event.

This belief is represented by the letters VP, as shown on a wall of Chartres Cathedral[35] (44). We can see the similarity between this VP symbol and the chrismon[36] mentioned on page 32.

Belief in the story of the Virgin giving birth to a child by the Druid Carnutes led some people to believe that Christ had Celtic roots. This is why we find representations of him with light-brown hair and beard and a European-style physiognomy.

(44) Le symbole VP dans la Cathédrale de Chartres.

---

35      We'll see later that part of the Versailles estate originally belonged to the diocese of Chartres, particularly where the Grand Canal was built.

36      Emperor Constantine introduced the Christian chrismon symbol in the 4th century. He wanted to find an emblem for Christianity that would break away from the images he associated with paganism. He therefore composed this symbol made up of the Greek letters X (ki) and P (ro), often accompanied by the letters alpha and omega.

## ISIS, THE NURSING MOTHER.

However, the origins of the Virgo Parituræ seem to go back even further, to Egypt.

*« In the past, the underground chambers of temples were home to statues of Isis, which, when Christianity was introduced into Gaul, became the Black Virgins that people today venerate with a special reverence... In his book De dictis Germanicis, the scholar Elias Schadius noted a similar inscription: Isidi, seu Virgini ex qua filius proditurus est (To Isis, or to the Virgin from whom the Son will be born). »*[37]

---

37      Fulcanelli, *Le Mystère des Cathédrales*, éditions Jean-Jacques Pauvert, 1973, ch 8

In an excellent article on Isis in Wikipedia, we can read the following:

*During the first four centuries of the Christian era, the maternal figures of Isis, mother of Horus, and Mary, mother of Jesus, coexisted. In Egypt and around the Mediterranean Sea, the cult of Isis flourished until the 4th century, and her figurations were widespread. The oldest known representation of the Mother of Christ is a painting in the catacomb of St. Priscilla in Rome, which may date from the 2nd century. The Virgin is seated, nursing her son, while a figure points to a star above her head... Now, Isis iconography very often shows the goddess seated on a throne nursing the very young Horus. This borrowing from Isiac cults is all the more likely given that Greco-Roman culture offers no other model of a breast-feeding goddess.*

The development of Sainte-Anne d'Auray as a place of pilgrimage, France's third-largest after Lourdes and Lisieux, began with a mysterious discovery in 1625. In the village of Ker Anna, six people, guided in the night by torches in the sky according to some, unearthed a highly degraded olive wood statuette of a woman breastfeeding two children. This representation was later remodeled by monks from Auray to depict Sainte-Anne with the Virgin Mary and the Infant Jesus on her lap.

The discovery of a very old statuette of a woman nursing her children in a place called Keranna creates a special link between Isis and Saint-Anne.

However, it is the origin of the city of Paris that is Isis' greatest influence in France. According to the clerics of the royal abbey of Saint-Germain-des-Prés in Paris, their abbey was founded on the site of a temple to Isis. Here is the oldest known mention of this thesis[38] :

*«This Isis was once worshipped by the people of the city of Lutetia, now known as Paris, in a place called Lutoticia, opposite the Mount of Mars. She can still be seen there today, and was worshipped and venerated by several Frankish pagan princes, including Francion, Pharamond, Merove and Childéric, right up to the time of Clovis, the first Christian.. »*

---

38      Note added to the chronicle De Gestis Francorum by the monk Aimoin (9th century), perhaps dating from the reign of Charles V (1364-1380).

This little note explains that the early kings of France worshipped the goddess Isis until their conversion to Christianity. It's quite possible that this veneration continued afterwards, but in a hidden way or transformed outwardly into adoration of the Virgin Mary.

*Saint-Germain-des-Prés Abbey is an ancient Benedictine abbey in Paris, founded in the mid-6th century by the Merovingian king Childebert I, son of Clovis, and the bishop of Paris, Saint Germain. Before the abbey was founded, there was already a temple in Roman times, probably dedicated to Isis, then called Locotice, which ensured immortality for initiates. This place of worship benefited from a slightly higher position than the surrounding area, sheltered from the annual floods and outside the wetlands known in the 10th century as the "Clos de Laas"* [39].

We therefore understand that this temple dedicated to Isis stood on a mound surrounded by marshy areas, flooded when the Seine flooded. It's the topographical peculiarity of solid ground emerging from wetlands in relation to Isis, as was the case with Sainte-Anne-la-Palud .

We know that Isis worship did not disappear with the arrival of Christianity.

---

39      Wikipedia, Saint-Germain-des-Près Abbey.

*Between the end of the Middle Ages and the middle of the 19th century, French and European scholars massively accepted and disseminated the idea that the founding of the city of Paris was linked to the cult of the goddess Isis. Based on the legendary statue of Isis in Saint-Germain-des-Prés, an etymology was developed that made Paris the city located near the Isis of Saint-Germain; the Latin word Parisis must have been derived from the expression Para Isis "which adjoins, which is near (the temple) of Isis"»*[40].

Whatever the reality of this version of the etymology of Paris, now very much in doubt, what's important for the present investigation is to know what Louis XIII and Louis XIV thought of it.  It is highly probable that they accepted this origin for the name of the city of Paris, as it was predominant in their day. As kings of France, they may also have been influenced by the beliefs of the early Merovingian kings.

A stela[41] dated 370 B.C. and discovered at Heliopolis, north-east of Cairo in Egypt, reads as follows:

*Isis was absent from the marshes of Chemnis, where she had taken refuge with Horus, when she returned to find her son lifeless. She called for help from the local peasants, who were powerless to help her. Selkis, the scorpion goddess, appeared in the meantime and advised Isis to invoke the Sun, whose boat was sailing in the sky. At Isis's call, the solar barque stopped. Thoth, the great magician-god, climbed down. He uttered a long incantation over Horus. When Horus was cured, Thot returned to inform the Sun, and the barque resumed its journey.*

This little anecdote about the life of Isis is full of interesting details. We see links established between Selkis, the Scorpion goddess, the marshes and the Sun riding in a boat. All this is to enable the child Horus to recover from an illness. Now, on November 1, in the sign of Scorpio, the Sun stops at its rising point in the axis of the Versailles marshes. Let's not forget that Louis XIV almost died at the age of 19 from typhoid fever, which he caught from infected water. It's only a short step from there to thinking he could have identified with the Egyptian god Horus.

---

40      Wikipedia, *Isis*

41      Metternich stele, lines 168 to 248, New York Museum

*On January 5, 1677, Jean-Baptiste Lully (1632-1687) presented King Louis XIV with a lyric tragedy entitled Isis, based on a libretto by Philippe Quinault (1635-1688). The story is inspired by the Greco-Roman myth of the nymph Io, mistress of Jupiter, who became a goddess in Egypt under the name of Isis. The opera ends in Egypt with Juno's forgiveness of Io and her apotheosis, transformation into an eternal divinity and acceptance among the sky gods as a goddess revered by the peoples of the Nile.*[42] :

**Final apotheosis**

*Juno's words:*

> *After a rigorous torture*
>
> *Taste the perfect gifts the Gods have chosen*
>
> *And under the new name of Isis*
>
> *Enjoy a happiness that never ends.*

*Words from Juno and Jupiter:*

> *Gods, receive Isis into the rank of the immortals!*
>
> *In the rank of the immortals.*
>
> *Peoples near the Nile, build her altars.*

*Words of the Egyptians:*

> *Come, come, new divinity,*
>
> *Isis, Isis, turn your eyes upon us,*
>
> *See the ardour of our zeal.*
>
> *The heavenly Court calls you,*
>
> *All in this place revere you,*
>
> *Isis, Isis is immortal,*
>
> *Isis will shine in this place.*
>
> *Isis rejoices with the Gods*
>
> *In eternal glory.*

---

42    Wikipedia, *Isis*

If the idea was to present this text to Louis XIV, it must have been well known that he would not be shocked by such eulogy of the goddess Isis and her acceptance into the Pantheon, he who decorated his château and gardens with representations of the gods of mythology. The opera was presented at the Château Neuf de Saint-Germain-en-Laye, as the Versailles Opera House did not yet exist in 1677. [43].

**_All in this place revere you..._**
**_Isis will shine in this place..._**

But what is this all about? What do these last words, this final apotheosis, refer to?

Could it be that the places mentioned in the apotheosis of this opera refer to the Château de Saint-Germain-en-Laye, or to Versailles, or even to the whole of the Paris region? After all, this is where the seat of the Kingdom of France is located. Let's take a closer look at these locations.

---

43      The Versailles Opera House was planned in 1682 and begun in 1685, but financial problems interrupted construction for almost a century. On May 16, 1770, the Opéra was inaugurated with a performance of Persée by Quinault and Lully, composed in 1682, who had also written the opera Isis.

# DOES VERSAILLES HAVE LINKS WITH OTHER CHÂTEAUX?

(47) THE CHÂTEAU NEUF DE SAINT-GERMAIN-DES-PRÉS, NOW DESTROYED, WITH ITS TERRACES AND GARDENS LEADING DOWN TO THE SEINE. SITUATED ON A HILL, ITS FACADE FACED DUE EAST, OFFERING A SPLENDID VIEW OF THE SEINE VALLEY AND THE PARIS BASIN. THE BUILDINGS WERE ALIGNED ON A NORTH-SOUTH AXIS. IN THE BACKGROUND, THE CHÂTEAU VIEUX, WITH THE HOLY CHAPEL SPIRE BEHIND IT.
A 17TH-CENTURY ENGRAVING BY CLAUDE CHASTILLON.

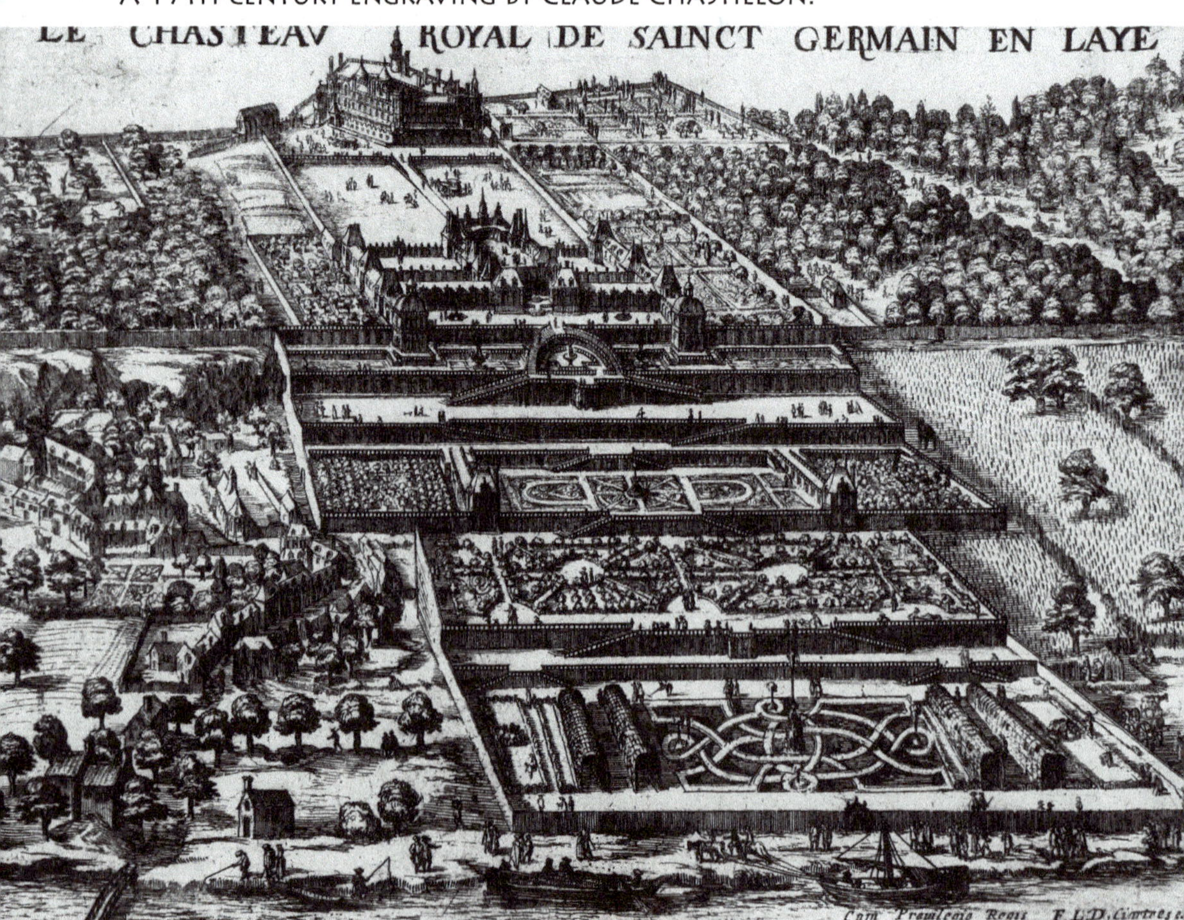

n September 5, 1638, the future King Louis XIV was born at the Château Neuf de Saint-Germain-en-Laye (47). On May 14, 1643, less than 5 years later, his father Louis XIII died on the same site. This magnificent château, begun by Henri II in 1557 and foreshadowing the wonders of Versailles, is now in ruins, sold after the French Revolution to the ancient steward Louis-Charles Guy (1742-1823), who demolished it, subdivided the land and sold the building materials.

We'll come back to this a little later. First, let's take a look at the site of the Château Vieux, whose origins are much more ancient.

*Saint-Germain-en-Laye owes its origins to the construction, by French king Robert II the Pious (972-1031), of a monastery dedicated to Saint Germain, probably Saint Germain de Paris, founder of the abbey of Saint-Germain-des-Prés, who lived nearby in the 6th century[44].*

This same Saint Germain, appointed bishop of Paris in 555 under the reign of Childebert I, is said to have founded his abbey on the site of an ancient temple of Isis, where initiates were assured immortality. The name Saint-Germain-en-Laye can be understood as "Saint-Germain-in-the-forest". The place thus mirrors Saint-Germain-des-Prés, "Saint-Germain-in-the-meadows", since meadows and forests are two opposite poles, one luminous, clear and safe, the other dark, secluded and dangerous. The forest is also the Druidic place par excellence, a symbol of the other world and a place of learning.

Around 1124, King Louis VI the Fat (1081-1137) had the first fortified castle of Saint-Germain-en-Laye built on the site of today's château, opposite the Saint-Germain priory. Saint Louis enlarged the castle and commissioned Pierre de Montreuil to build one of the first Holy Chapels, completed in 1238. The same architect is also said to have built the Chapel of the Blessed Virgin in the Abbey of Saint-Germain-des-Prés.

Now, a quick look at Google Earth shows that the axis of the church at Saint-Germain-des-Prés is aimed exactly at the Sainte Chapelle of the Château Vieux de Saint-Germain-en-Laye and, beyond that, at the church (48). The axis is inclined 15.61° north of east.

---

44      Historical dictionary of the Paris area by Dr Ermete Pierotti

On August 15, 1346, during the Hundred Years' War, the "Black Prince", son of King Edward III of England, took the town of Saint-Germain-en-Laye, looting and burning it and the château, which was destroyed except for the Holy Chapel. Twenty years later, under Charles V, it was rebuilt and transformed into a fortress. From 1417 to 1440, the château was occupied by the English. When François I married Claude de France in the Holy Chapel on May 18, 1514, the château became the king's favorite residence. It's clear, then, that this was a much-coveted location, but for reasons that aren't very explicit.

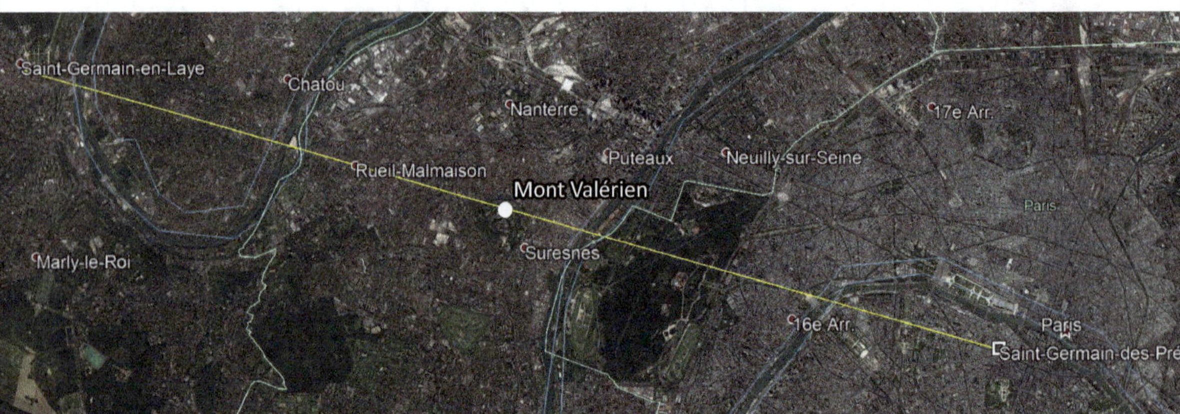


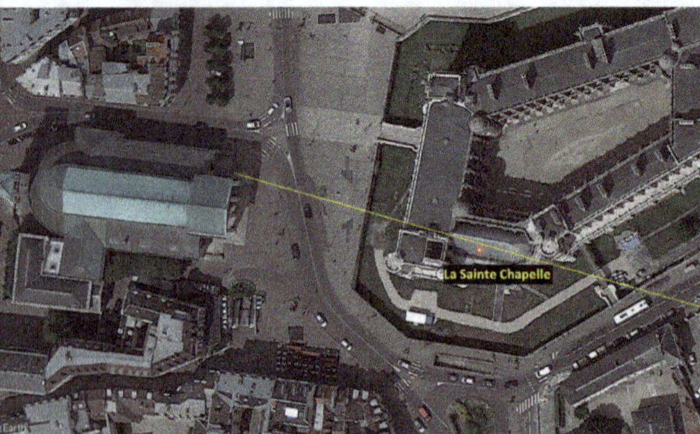


Saint-Germain-en-Laye

Saint-Germain-des-Prés

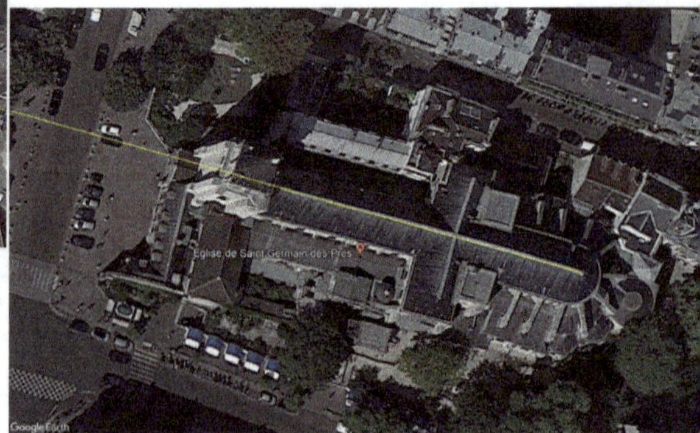


(48) THE LINK BETWEEN THE TWO SAINT-GERMAINS: MEADOWS AND FOREST. THE LOWER RIGHT IMAGE SHOWS THE EXACT ORIENTATION OF THE CHURCH OF SAINT-GERMAIN-DES-PRÉS TOWARDS THE HOLY CHAPEL AND THE CHURCH OF SAINT-GERMAIN-EN-LAYE. THE UPPER IMAGE GIVES AN OVERALL VIEW OVER A DISTANCE OF 1,895 METERS. MONT VALÉRIEN (SURESNES) CAN BE SEEN HALF-WAY BETWEEN THE TWO.

Exactly halfway between the two Saint-Germains lies Mont Valérien (h. 123 m), where Louis XIII had chapels built along a Way of the Cross that climbed to the summit. From here, both Saint-Germains are easily visible. (49).

A very special relationship seems to situate Versailles in this ensemble, for between the abbey of Saint-Germain-des-Prés and the center of the Grand Canal we have an axis exactly symmetrical to the one that joins the two Saint-Germains, 15.61° south of west (50). The Grand Canal lies to the south of Saint-Germain-en-Laye, and we'll see just how precisely.

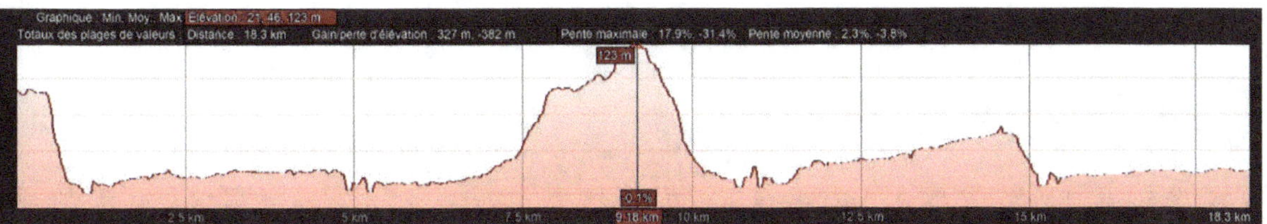

(49) Profile of the topography between the two Saint-Germains. In the center, Mont Valérien provides a view of both locations.

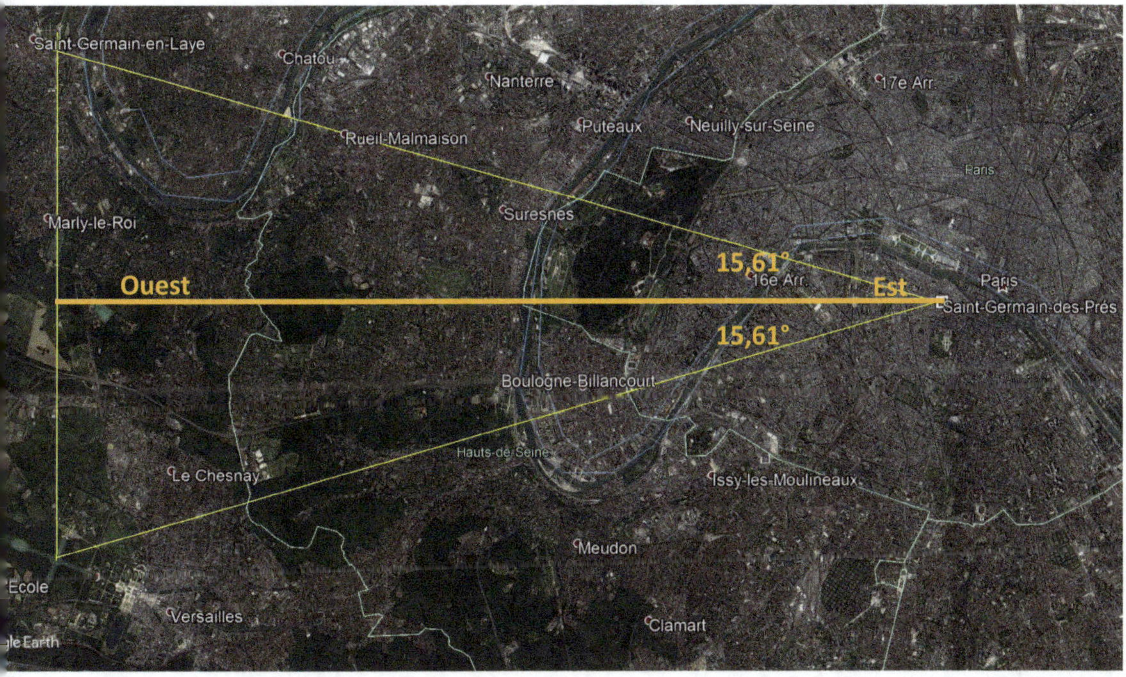

(50) A symmetrical relationship around the Saint-Germain-des-Prés parallel situates the Château de Saint-Germain-en-Laye and the center of the Grand Canal de Versailles. A 10 km north-south line links this point to the gardens of Château de Saint-Germain-en-Laye, passing through the Grand Miroir basin at Château de Marly-le-Roi.

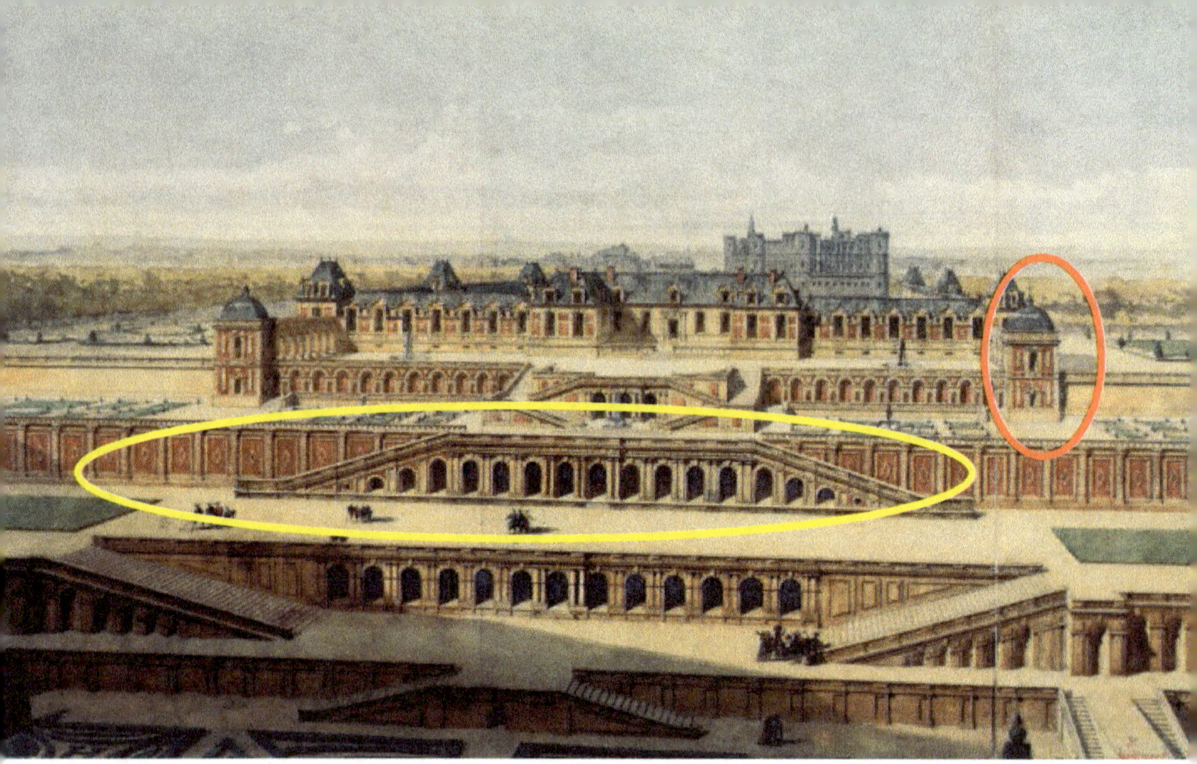

(51) The Château Neuf de Saint-Germain-en-Laye in 1637 painted by Auguste Alexandre Guillaumot. Remains still visible today near the D190 road are circled in yellow. They show the exact position of the buildings. A remaining tower, preserved in the hotel-restaurant "Le Pavillon Henri IV", is circled in red.


(52) A few remains of the Château-neuf can be found near the road D190 at Saint-Germain-en-Laye. The elements circled in yellow in figure (51) can be identified here. (BELOW) The brick panels and ramp on the left (OPPOSITE) The 13 arcades under the walkway between the two ramps.

To do this, I need to put the Château Neuf back on the map, as I haven't found any illustrations of the ground plan. Figure (51) shows the splendour of this château, now forgotten even by the people who live there. We can see how the château's central axis is located just to the left (south) of the Château Vieux, shown in grey in the background. The axis still exists. It's the Rue Thiers. On the right, you can see gardens that still exist. The courtyard in front of the château faces east, with a view of Paris. The north and south sides are partially enclosed by an arcaded structure ending in two towers. This structure is reminiscent of the arcades in the Peristyle of the Château du Trianon, designed by Louis XIV to allow the axis to continue through the building. These arcades in the Saint-Germain château are exactly on the north-south axis leading to Versailles.

On site, there are still a few remnants of this place, which, had it been preserved, would be almost on a par with Versailles:

- in the area circled in yellow in figure (51), at a place called "La rampe des grottes" near the road D190 (52).

- the hotel-restaurant "Le Pavillon Henri IV", which retains the right-hand tower that was part of the structure that framed the courtyard in front of the château.

- in the gardens on the other side of the road D190, on the descent towards the Seine, there are remnants of the formal gardens.

Using the "Portrait des châteaux royaux de Saint-Germain-en-Laye en 1614 (BnF) Alessandro Francini (drawing) Michel Lasne (engraver)", I was able to superimpose the image on the Google Earth satellite image, adjusting the size of the gardens and the château to suit the perspective. (53).

**The perfectly north-south axis running from the center of the Grand Canal de Versailles arrives exactly in the main part of the Château-Neuf.**

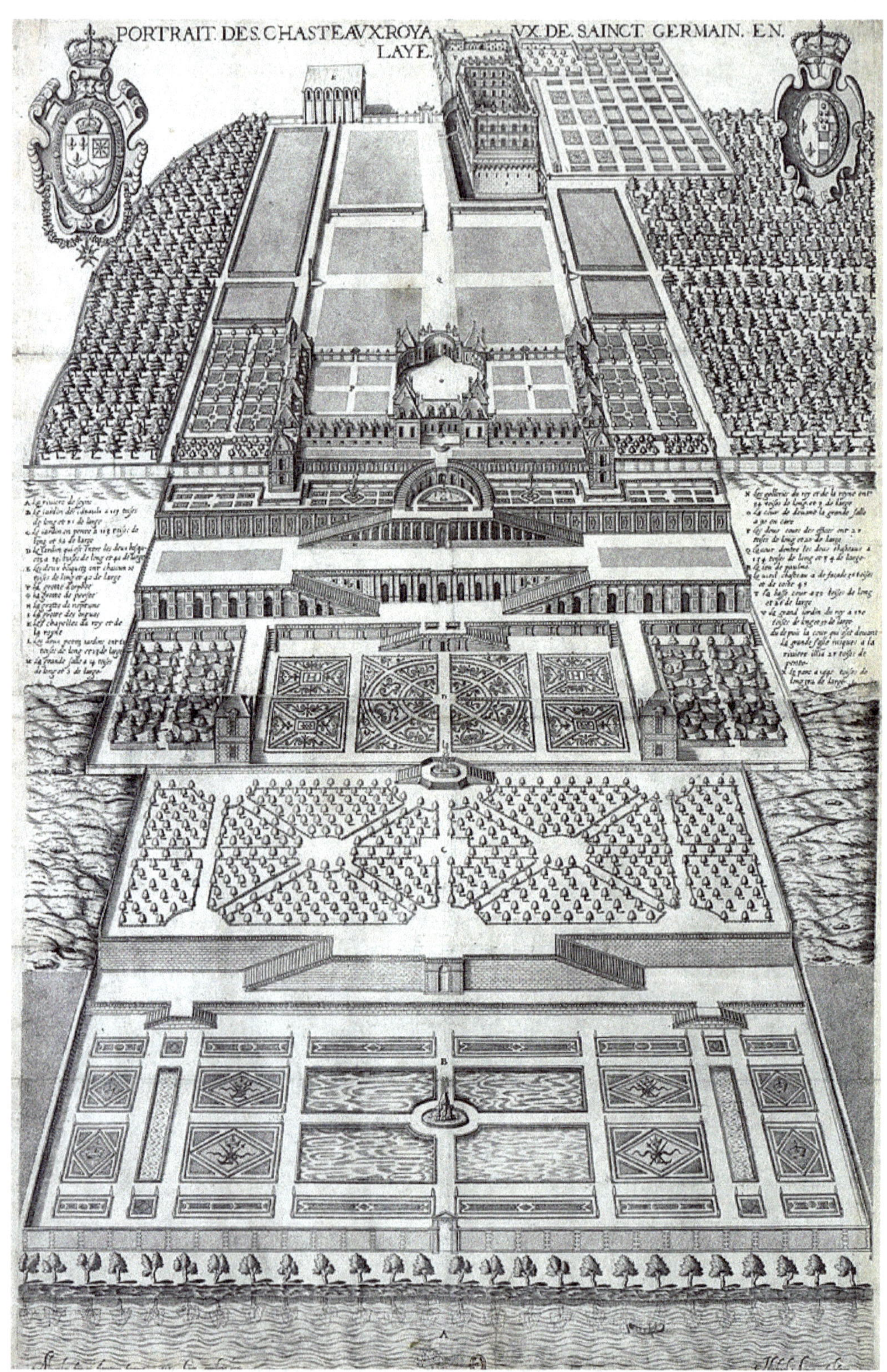

PORTRAIT. DES. CHASTEAVX ROYA VX DE. SAINCT. GERMAIN. EN. LAYE.

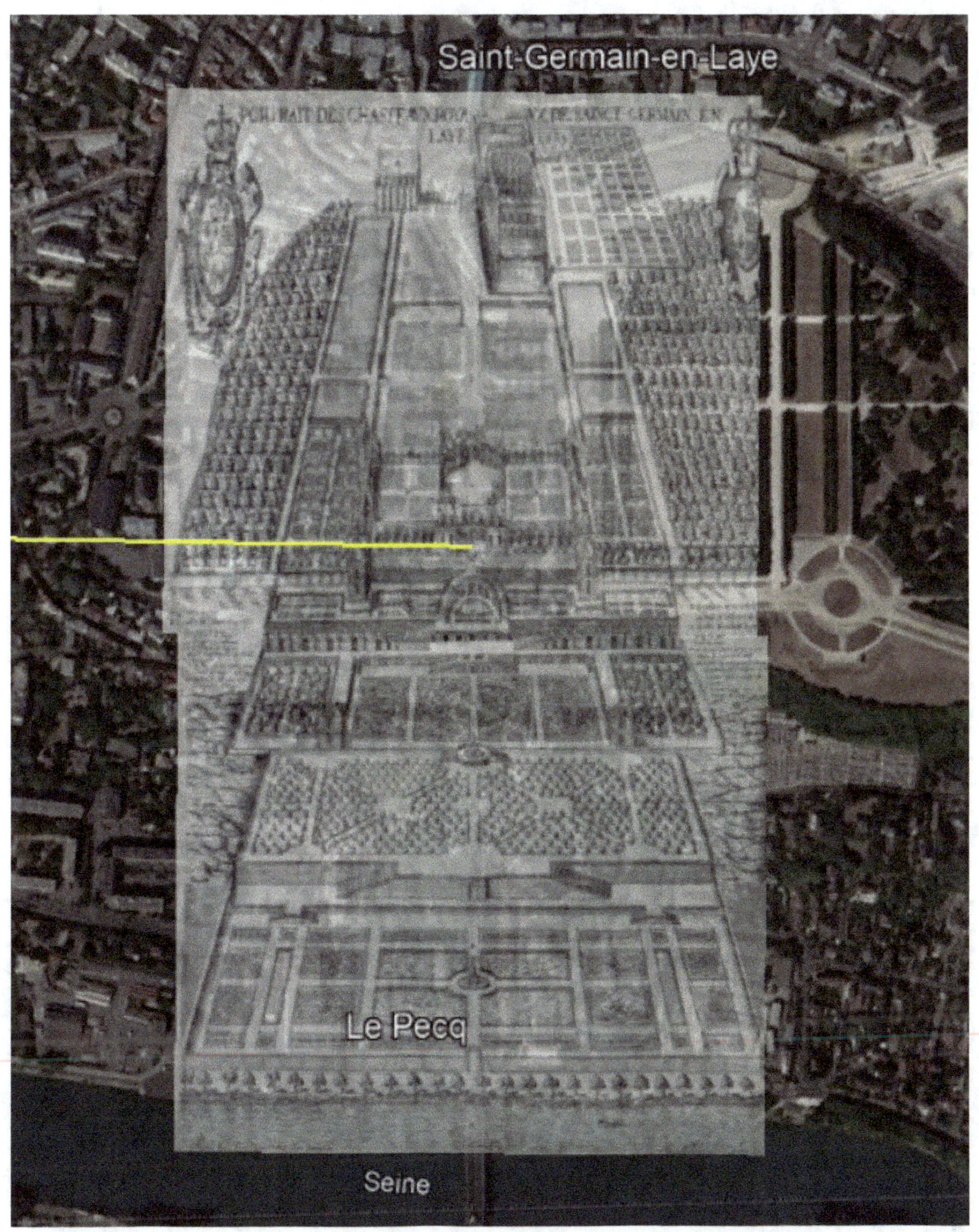


(53) (Above) The engraving superimposed on the satellite image of the site. The yellow line is the perfectly north-south axis running from the center of the Grand Canal de Versailles to the main part of the Château Neuf.                    (Opposite) the engraving of the two royal châteaux in Saint-Germain-en-Laye in 1614 (BNF) by Alessandro Francini (dessin) and Michel Lasne (graveur)".

(54) (LEFT) THE NORTH-SOUTH AXIS BETWEEN SAINT-GERMAIN-EN-LAYE AND VERSAILLES PASSES THROUGH THE GRAND MIROIR LAKE AT CHÂTEAU DE MARLY.

(55) (BELOW) THE TRIANON AXIS (IN RED) LIES EXACTLY BETWEEN THE TWO LINES LINKING VERSAILLES TO SAINT-GERMAIN-DES-PRÉS AND TO THE NORTH TO MARLY AND THE CHÂTEAU NEUF AT SAINT-GERMAIN-EN-LAYE.

(56) (below) The north-south axis of the center of the Grand Canal (yellow line) runs exactly in line with the main body of the Château Neuf de Saint-Germain-en-Laye. I've positioned the château, outlined in white and surrounded by red, its terrace ("blackened") and the stairs leading down to the ramp according to all the elements at my disposal: Château Vieux, plans, drawings, remains... To the right of the photograph is a formal garden in the same position as in figure (53). The courtyard of the hotel "Le Pavillon Henri IV" stands on the site of the château courtyard. Rue Thiers follows the central axis to the south of the Château Vieux.

This north-south axis cuts exactly across the end of the fountain at the western end of the Trianon axis. It passes through the Grand Miroir of Château de Marly (54).

The axis coming from Saint-Germain-des-Prés passes exactly through the south-east entrance gate of the Château du Trianon before arriving at the Grand Canal.

This set of verifiable facts points to a real landscape intention for the establishment of the royal châteaux in relation to Saint-Germain. This process seems to have begun as early as the 6th century, under the impetus of the Merovingian kings, particularly Clovis.

In the second volume of this book, I will return to the details of this geometry, and in particular to the central shape of the Grand Canal, which demonstrates geometric and metrological knowledge that defies the imagination.

I can't help but wonder about the name of the Parisian soccer team, which is known the world over: Paris Saint-Germain. Clearly, the destinies of these two places are closely linked.

By establishing this site, Louis XIV was simply continuing the practices of his ancestors, introduced by the Gauls. A book by Bernard Robreau[45] sums up the current state of knowledge on this forgotten ancient science.

*The Druids most likely knew a sacred art of geography that allowed them to speculate not only "on the dimensions of the world and of the earth»[46], but also to determine the sites of Gallo-Roman towns in a pre-scientific way.»*

He continues further on[47]

*« The Gauls may well have constructed space mathematically. Our hagiographic studies had led us to suspect this several times. C. Jullian implicitly admits it, the Welsh text of Lludd and Llevelys seems to have memorized it, and both Caesar (the criers) and Raoul de Presles (fires and no doubt smoke) indicate two ways in which they transmitted information. Surveying was not unknown to them either, as B. Liger's[48] work on Carnute land plots has shown. The fact that the Romans borrowed the names of leagues and arpents also points to their expertise in this area. »*

We may be sceptical about the accuracy of these settlements at such an early date, as we tend to see the Gauls as utterly primitive. But the facts are there. On the relative position of the Butte de Rochefort with the extremities of Gaul, Bernard Robreau writes[49]

*« The precision is absolutely astounding, and helps convince us that the Gauls really were capable of calculating where the center of their nation was. »*

---

45    Bernard Robreau, *Les Carnutes et le centre de la Gaule*, Société archéologique d'Eure-et-Loir, 1997, page 1

46    Julius Cesar, *The Gallic Wars,* VI, 14

47    idem, page 18

48    B. Liger, *Les parcellaires et réseaux routiers en Beauce de Mer à Patay*, 1974

49    idem, page 31

In my previous books, I've shown how this very precise surveying of space goes all the way back to the Megalithic period, around 5000 BC. It is clear that megalithic scholars already knew the exact dimensions of the Earth. This science must have been passed down from generation to generation by initiates, in an oral tradition. The druids didn't write, as they didn't want to fix their thoughts in something immobile, preferring to look into the eyes of the person to whom they were passing on their knowledge.

Following on from his findings, Bernard Robreau writes[50] :

*« In this way, we discover that in Northern Gaul, many city capitals were not located at random, but according to strictly calculated locations, which were probably determined within the framework of a sacred geography and tended to implant them in places charged with beneficial power. »*

We can therefore assume that this principle was re-established following the fall of the Roman Empire, and that it is entirely logical that the settlement of the first kings of France was based on these principles.

The first Merovingian king was Childéric I, born around 436 and who died in 481, king of the Salian Franks from 457 or 458. His name, made up of the Frankish elements hild- "combat" and -rīk "powerful", is attested in the Latinized form Childericus. He was the father of Clovis I.

Clovis was known as Hlodowig, meaning "glorious in battle". Born around 466 and dying in Paris in 511, he was king of the Salian Franks, then king of all the Franks from 481 to 511, a total of 30 years. He was the first Christian king of the Frankish kingdom.

### Now, Hlodowig gives Ludovico in Latin,which is Louis!

All the French kings named Louis thus follow in the footsteps of Clovis, who was initially a follower of Druidic philosophy.

After Clovis, Childebert I was King of the Franks of Paris from 511 to 558, a total of 47 years. Between Clovis and Childebert, therefore, there were 77 years of reign, a great period of stability enabling the settlement of Paris.

It is therefore quite conceivable that the site of the Château de Versailles was identified by the druid surveyors long before the first stone was laid, due to its orientation and marshlands, which may explain why it belonged to the diocese of Chartres[51].

---

50     idem, page 42

51     See "Appendix 4. The Chartres diocese and Jean-François de Gondi", page 122

In developing his estate at Versailles, Louis XIII was pursuing a project that had perhaps begun long before him.

To support this idea, let's take a detour to 6th-century Paris..

(57) THE PORTE SAINT-DENIS IN PARIS WITH THE INSCRIPTION LUDOVICO MAGNO.

(58) STATUE OF LOUIS XIV ON HORSEBACK, PLACE VENDÔME, PARIS, WITH THE INSCRIPTION LUDOVICO MAGNO. ENGRAVING BY PIERRE LEPAUTRE, 1699.

# Louis XIV and the Founding Abbeys of Paris



(59) The axis of the church Saint Germain l'Auxerrois, aiming at the Holy Chapel in Saint-Germain-en-Laye.

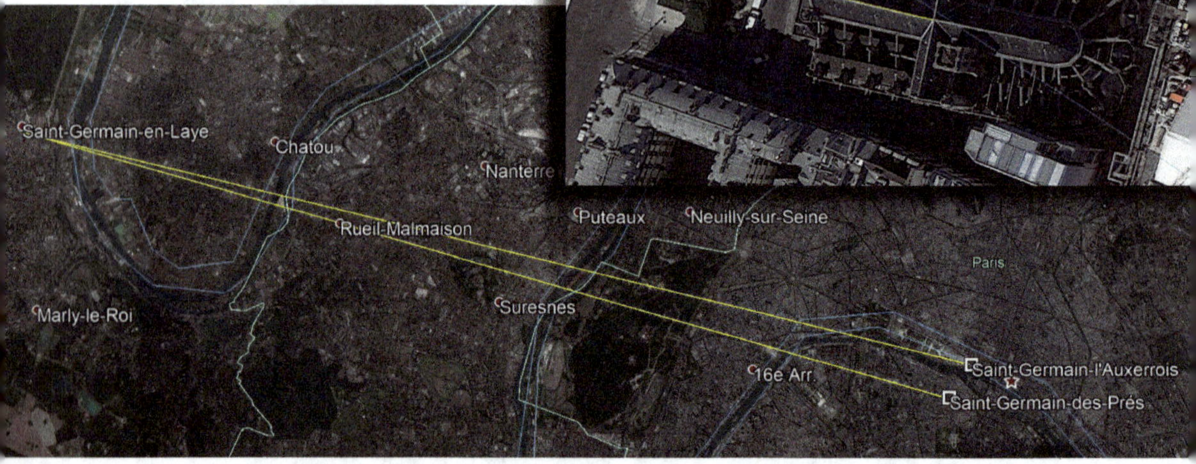

(60) (Below) Map of Paris under the Romans with the Cardo Maximus.

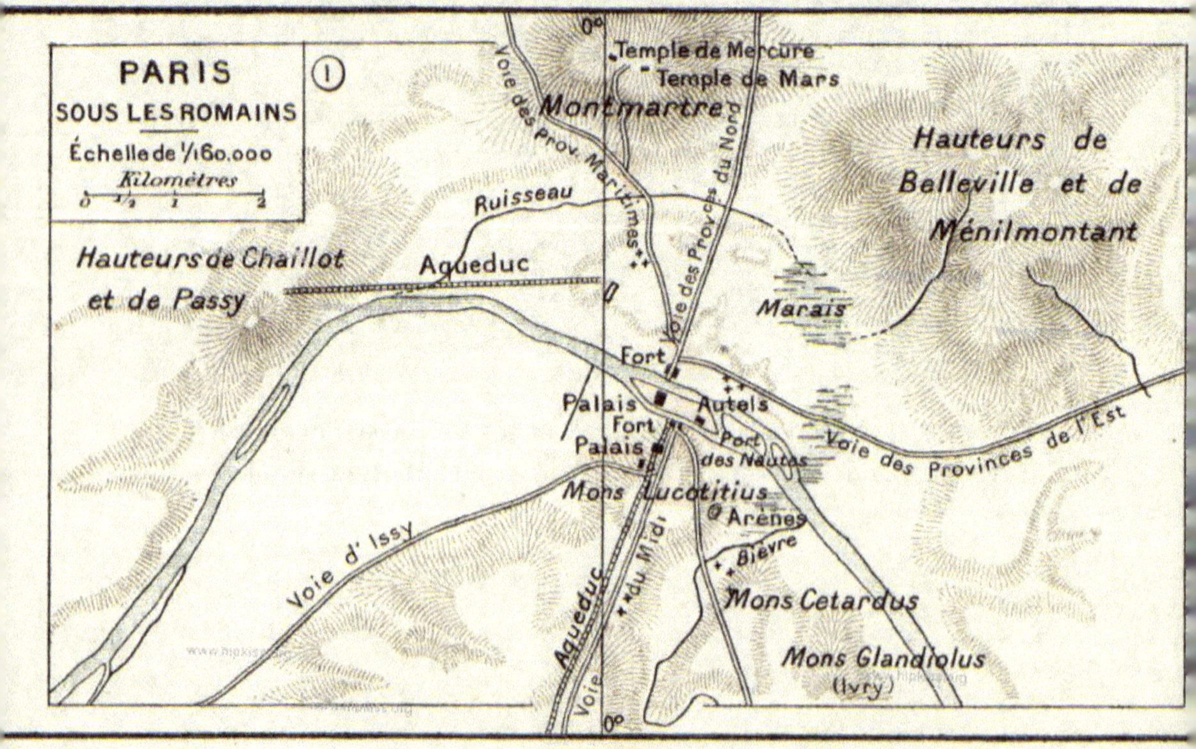

The Gallia Christiana states that in 581 there were four abbeys at the gates of Paris: Saint-Laurent to the east, Sainte-Geneviève to the south, Saint-Germain-des-Prés to the west and Saint-Germain-l'Auxerrois to the north.

First, we turn our attention to a church dedicated to a different Saint Germain: Saint-Germain-l'Auxerrois (380 - 448), a building whose origins date back to the 7th century and which lies just south-east of the Louvre. Our thesis is confirmed by the fact that, once again, its axis is aimed at the Holy Chapel in Saint-Germain-en-Laye.

Of the four named abbeys, only one is dedicated to a woman. The abbey of Sainte-Geneviève was founded in 502 (originally called the monastery of the Holy Apostles) by Clovis and his wife Clotilde on the mons Lucotitius, today's Sainte-Geneviève mountain. Once again, this site dedicated to a female figure is on a high point, as was the temple of Isis. When Sainte-Geneviève died in 512, her remains were buried in the abbey church alongside Clovis, and later joined by Queen Clotilde.

Geneviève, who knew Saint Germain-l'Auxerrois, originally had a Celtic name, Genovefa. In Breton, genoù is the word for mouth and eff "heaven", genoueff would mean " mouth of heaven " or " opening to heaven ". Another interpretation would give Genovefa as a name derived from the Old French kenowifa, a feminine Germanic name that splits into ken- "to know" (kennen in German, ken in Scottish) and wifa "woman" (wife in English, Weib in German), which gives "woman (or wife) of knowledge". In the end, these two interpretations come down to the same meaning: she who has espoused knowledge, who is open to the Spirit. The Sainte-Geneviève library, which was part of the abbey, was once the third largest library in Europe, and still exists today as a university library.

Previously, the summit was topped by the central building of Roman Lutetia, the Forum, now replaced by the Henri-IV high school[52] and beside it is the Panthéon[53] and the Sorbonne, the major university of Paris. So we understand that Mont Sainte-Geneviève, a feminine place, is the original heart of Paris. We can see that the marshes reached the foot of mons Lucotitius to the east. (60)

---

52      The Sainte-Geneviève abbey has been incorporated into the Henri IV school buildings.

53      The Pantheon was originally another majestic St. Genevieve church, built by Louis XV in 1744. Next door is the church of Saint-Etienne du Mont, dedicated in 1626 during the reign of Louis the Just by Jean-François de Gondi, first archbishop of Paris and owner of Versailles before its sale to King Louis XIII.

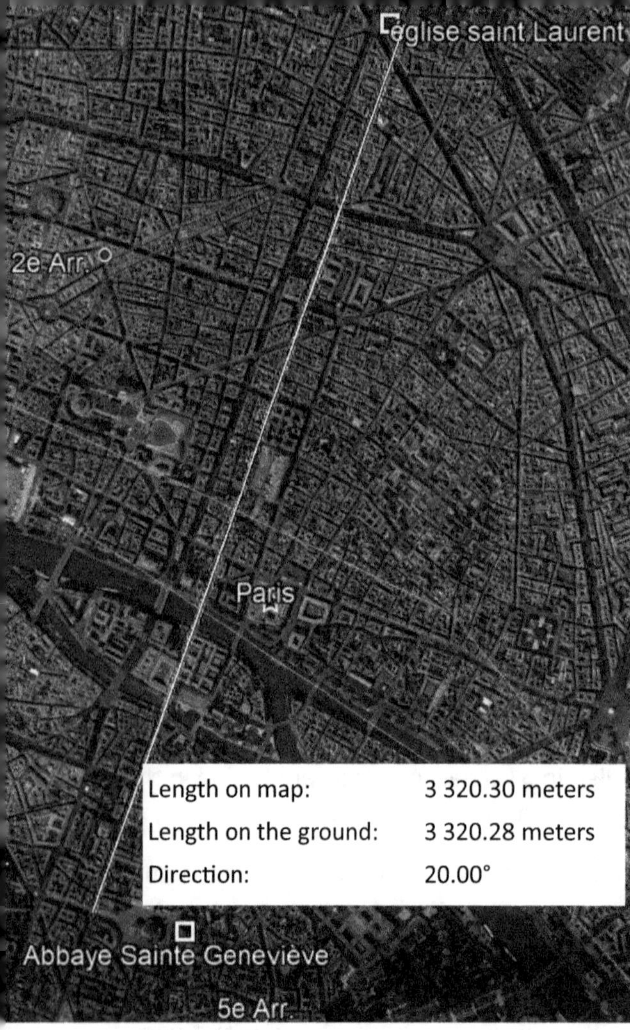




This hill was the starting point of the Roman Cardo Maximus, the main street running north-south, which descended to cross the Seine on the Isle of the City (Île de la Cité) before heading up the present-day Rue Saint Martin. The word cardo gave rise to the word "cardinal" and its use for the cardinal axes, north, south, east and west. Here, the Cardo Maximus is clearly not north-south.

In fact, it runs perfectly straight for 3320 meters. It begins at the foot of Mont Sainte-Geneviève with rue Saint Jacques, which leads down to the Isle of the City, crossing the Seine once via the Petit-Pont.

(62) THE PORTE SAINT-MARTIN, BUILT IN 1674. THE BELL TOWER AND CHOIR OF SAINT-LAURENT CHURCH CAN BE SEEN IN THE DISTANCE THROUGH THE ARCHWAY.

After crossing the Isle of the City via rue de la Cité, it crosses the river a second time via the Pont Notre-Dame, before taking rue Saint-Martin. Arriving at Porte Saint-Martin (62), it runs straight under the gate and continues along rue du Faubourg Saint-Martin to the church of Saint Laurent. It is inclined at precisely 20° east of north-east.

*The Porte Saint-Martin is a Paris landmark, located on the site of an ancient gate in Charles V's city walls. It was erected in 1674 by order of Louis XIV, in honor of his victories on the Rhine and in Franche-Comté, by architect Pierre Bullet, a pupil of François Blondel, architect of the neighboring Porte Saint-Denis. The current monument, the fourth of its kind, is an 18-meter-high triumphal arch.*[54]

At the bottom of the engraving (62) is the text :

*The Porte Saint-Martin was built in place of the earlier one in 1674. It is 54 feet long.  The middle opening is 18 by 40 feet.*

---

54        Wikipedia.

(63) THE PORTE SAINT-MARTIN IN OUR TIME. NOTE THAT THE CENTRAL VAULT IS COMPOSED OF 23 STONES AND THE SIDE VAULTS OF 13 STONES EACH.

Louis XIV put his signature on this ancient axis of Paris. The geometry and measurements of this gate will be discussed later in this book.

This large offset of the axis from geographic north is surely deliberate, even if its orientation is partly determined by the axis of the Seine at this point. Its value of 20° is equal to the 18th part of a circle, and recalls the principle of dividing the circle into nine, dear to the Druids and present in the Celtic calendar (33).

In the Gallia Christiana, Saint-Laurent marked the East and Sainte-Geneviève the South, while Saint-Germain-l'Auxerrois marked the North, which is far from reality. On the contrary, there's a special relationship between Sainte-Geneviève and Saint-Germain-l'Auxerrois, as the angle between them is exactly that of a triple square placed on the cardinal axes (64).

The triple square or tri-square is one of the fundamental shapes used by megalithic surveyors to lay out monuments in the Carnac region. It's a simple geometric shape composed of 3 squares placed side by side. Its sides therefore have a ratio of 1 to 3. The angle of its diagonal to its side (18.435°) is exactly half the angle of a 3-4-5 triangle (36.87°), another major shape in use since Neolithic times.

(64) THE TRIPLE SQUARE PLACED ON THE PRECISE CARDINAL AXES LINKING THE CHURCHES OF "ST. GENEVIEVE" AND "SAINT-GERMAIN-L'AUXERROIS". THE GIVEN DIRECTION OF 341.57° = 360° - 18.43°. TAN (18.43°) = 1/3.

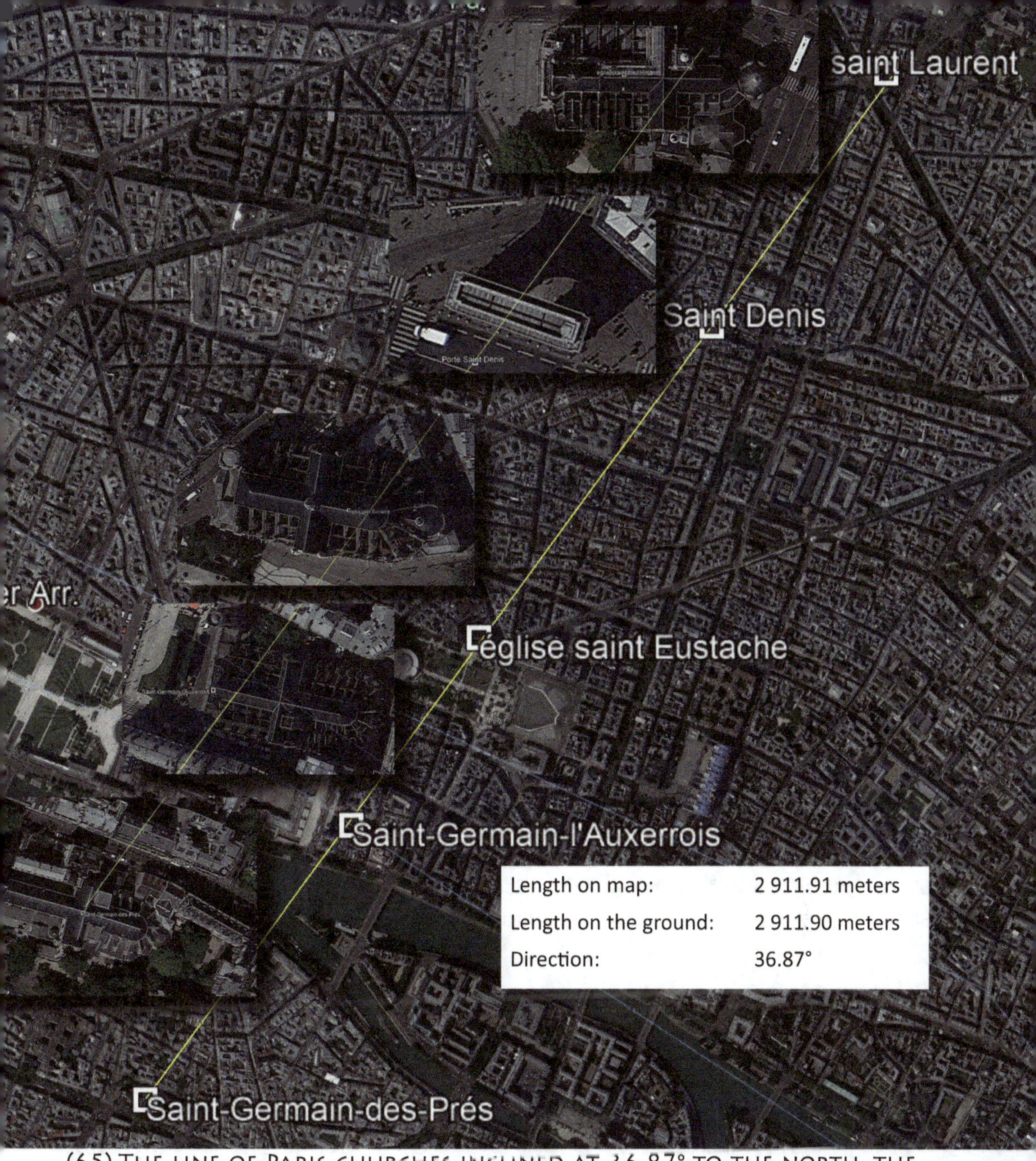




Now, three of the four abbeys that bounded Paris - Saint-Laurent, Saint-Germain-l'Auxerrois and Saint-Germain-des-Prês - are actually positioned on a straight line that is inclined at precisely the angle of a 3-4-5 triangle with respect to north (65). This line runs from the transepts of Saint-Germain-des-Prês in the south to the transepts of Saint-Laurent in the north. Another church, Saint-Eustache, also joins the line.

But the most astonishing thing about this geometry is the fact that this line runs precisely through the center of the Porte Saint Denis, built in 1672 by the architect François Blondel, to the glory of Louis XIV.  It stands on the site of a Paris gateway in the ancient Charles V city walls, at the end of rue Saint-Denis and the start of rue du Faubourg Saint-Denis.

*The Porte Saint-Denis is a triumphal arch inspired by the Arch of Titus in Rome. Auguste Choisy, in his History of Architecture, gives the composition of the Porte Saint-Denis, based on the division of a square into twos and threes. The monument is 24.65 meters wide, 25 meters high and 5 meters thick. The arcade is 15.35 meters high under the arch and 8 meters wide; the small doors are 3.30 meters by 1.70 meters.[55]*

The Arch of Titus in Rome measures 13.50 meters wide by 15.42 meters high, giving a ratio of 8:7, which corresponds to the ratio between a pillar and its shadow at Trianon latitude[56].

However, it's the gate's measurements that are most astonishing, as it appears to have been accomplished using the meter, despite the fact that this was some 100 years before the French Revolution and the introduction of this length as a universal measure. The height of this door is given as 25 meters and its thickness as 5 meters.

---

55      https://fr.wikipedia.org/wiki/Porte_Saint-Denis
56      See "Appendix 2. Equinoxes and latitudes.", page 115

(66) THE PORTE SAINT-DENIS WAS BUILT DURING THE REIGN OF LOUIS XIV (1672). ITS HEIGHT OF 25.00 METERS, ITS THICKNESS OF 5.00 METERS AND ITS OPENING OF 8.00 METERS LEAVE LITTLE DOUBT THAT THE METER WAS USED AS A BASIC MEASUREMENT. NOW, WE'RE MORE THAN A CENTURY BEFORE THE FRENCH REVOLUTION AND THE OFFICIAL INTRODUCTION OF THIS MEASURE!

This is a ratio of 1 to 5, known as a quintuple square. Now, a quintuple square with measurements in units of 5 meters would seem to be a deliberate choice. The opening of the arch is given as 8 meters wide, while its height is 15.35 meters. We therefore understand that the measurements given are precise. They are not rounded. The conclusion seems obvious: the meter measure was well known in Louis XIV's time and used by his architects in their constructions. We'll come back to this in Volume 2.

Although this information may seem very hard to accept, the facts that follow will confirm this conclusion in breathtaking fashion.

We've just looked at two gates, Saint-Denis and Saint-Martin, built respectively by architect Francis Blondel and his pupil Pierre Bullet in 1672 and 1674. These two gates were built on the orders of Louis XIV himself. They are not very far apart. By examining the relationship between them, we'll discover siting principles that date back to Neolithic times, and which clearly make use of the meter.

These two doors are identically oriented. What's more, they are aligned with each other. But the axis connecting them is not exactly perpendicular to the streets' axes.

(67) PORTE SAINT-DENIS (LEFT) AND PORTE SAINT-MARTIN (RIGHT) ARE EQUAL-LY ORIENTED AND ALIGNED WITH EACH OTHER.

When we measure the angle of this alignment in relation to the East-West axis, we discover an angle of 18.44 degrees, the exact angle of the diagonal of a triple square. The distance between the west side of the Porte Saint-Denis and the east side of the Porte Saint-Martin, i.e. a line encompassing both monuments, is precisely 253 meters.

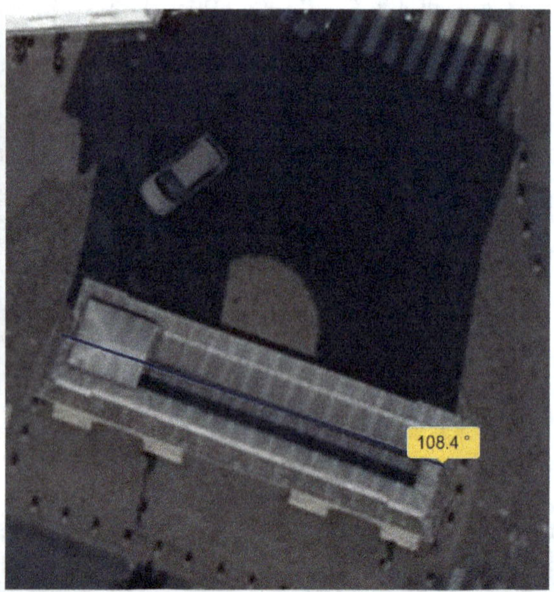


(68) Portes Saint-Denis and Saint-Martin are oriented at 18.43° south of the east-west axis, 108.43° from the north.

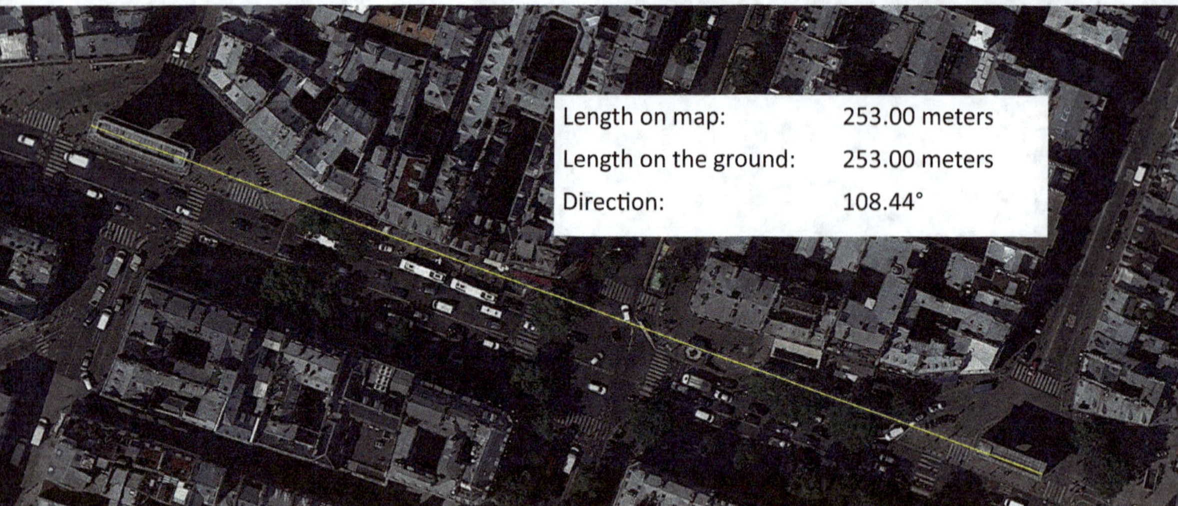


This line is inclined on the diagonal of a triple square. Numerically, therefore, its value is equal to the square root of 10, which is a so-called irrational number with an infinite number of digits after the decimal point.

It's this kind of number that turns off many math students when they're at school. This was also the case in ancient times, which is why the famous Pythagorean triangles, which have whole numbers on all 3 sides, including the diagonal, were very popular. Integers are things we can count and therefore understand, whereas irrational numbers are intangible. But let's get back to our study of the relationship between these two Louis XIV doors.

The length of the short side of the triple square that joins them is therefore equal to 253 meters divided by the square root of $10$[57]. So you'd expect a value followed by lots of decimal digits. But that's not the case, as the result is 80.00 meters[58], or 10 times the opening of the Porte Saint-Denis!

(69) GEOMETRY OF THE PORTES DE PARIS TRIPLE SQUARE USING THE METER.

**Can we therefore understand that the distance separating them was precisely chosen using a whole number of meters, 253, to deliver a whole number of meters on the sides, 80 for the short side and 240 for the long side of this triple square?**

The number 253 isn't entirely insignificant either, since it's equal to 23 x 11. Now, let's not forget that the Porte-Saint-Martin arch was divided into 23 parts, which isn't an easy division to make. Could this be an indication of geometry being used?

---

57      According to the Pythagorean theorem, the square of the diagonal is equal to the sum of the squares of the other two sides. So, for a triple square, $1^2 + 3^2 = 10$. The diagonal therefore has a value of the square root of 10, which can be written $\sqrt{10}$.

58      $253 / \sqrt{10} = 80.00562$, only 5 millimeters difference over 80m.

If we divide a circle into 23 equal parts, each segment produced will open up an angle of 15.65 degrees. Here, we're very close to the angle that connects the church of Saint-Germain-des-Prés with Saint-Germain-en-Laye on one side and Versailles on the other, an angle we've determined to be 15.61 degrees.

Another intriguing fact is the exact position of the Porte Saint-Denis on the abbey line. Close examination shows it to be exactly one third of the distance between the church of Saint-Laurent and the church of Saint-Germain-l'Auxerrois. This peculiarity led me to reposition the triple square so that one of its diagonals lies on the line of the abbeys, while the other runs north-south. This is possible because the angle formed by



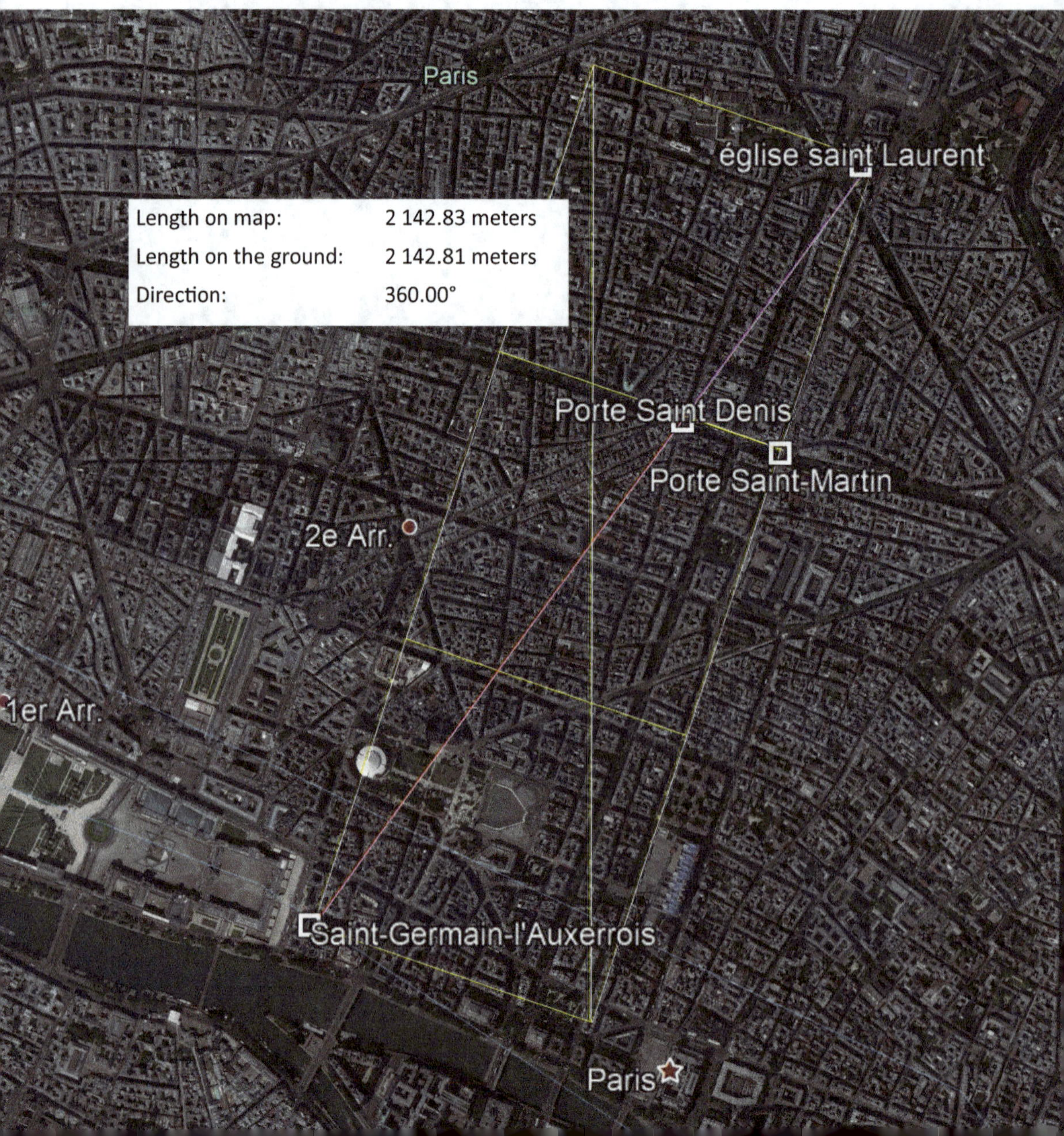

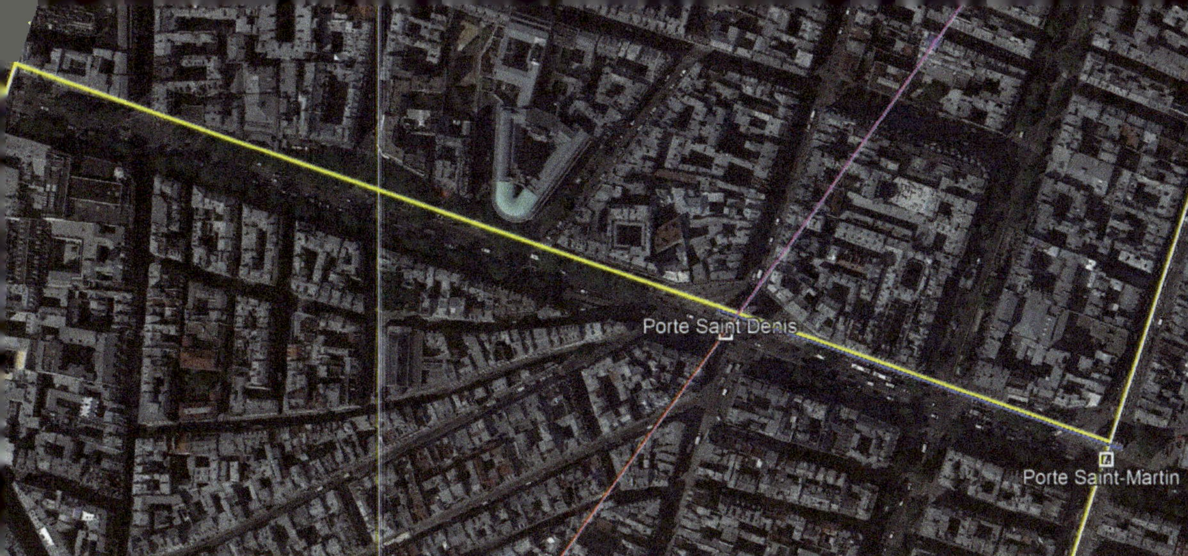




(71) THE SAINT-DENIS AND SAINT-MARTIN GATES MARK PRECISELY THE LOWER LINE OF THE FIRST SQUARE. THE PORTE SAINT-DENIS MARKS THE INTERSECTION OF THIS LINE WITH THE DIAGONAL.

the crossing of the diagonals of a triple square is equal to 2 x 18.435° or 36.87°, which is exactly the angle of the abbey line. Here we can see that the line marking the bottom of the upper square coincides perfectly with the axis of the Saint-Denis and Saint-Martin gates.

The length of the diagonal of this triple square will next attract our attention: 2142.85m.

The distance between Saint-Laurent church and the Porte Saint-Denis = 1/3 of this distance, i.e. 714.28 meters. The remaining distance between the Porte Saint-Denis and the crest of the roof of the Eglise Saint-Germain-l'Auxerrois is twice this distance, i.e. 1428.57 meters. Now this distance is exactly 10,000 meters divided by 7. This is further confirmation, if any were needed, of the use of the meter in the organization of Paris. But it's clear that this organization began long before the arrival of Louis XIV.

We can also see that the intersection of the two diagonals is right next to the Rue Réaumur, which cuts our triple square in two. Remember that Auguste Choisy said that the Porte Saint-Denis was based on the division of a square by 2 and by 3. It would seem that the major streets were organized in the same way. Another axis runs from the Porte Saint-Denis to the center of the Palais Royal garden, but this is where we'll end our exploration of Paris.

# The hidden science of Versailles

(72) The Orangery at the Château de Versailles by Étienne Allegrain in 1695.

A rmed now with the information that Louis XIV and his architects used modular geometry and the meter to make large-scale layouts, we'll be able to return to Versailles to better understand the designs they implanted in these very inhospitable marshlands.

This gigantic geometry, inscribed in the landscape and hitherto unknown, will be dealt with in the second volume of this book. It will reveal the principles and thought processes used by the designers of what is today one of the wonders of the world. Although this is not complex mathematics, it may seem daunting to some readers, who have been put off such matters by a school education that didn't suit them. That's why I've decided to put these elements in a separate book. To these people, I can suggest that they try to follow the conclusions without necessarily trying to understand all the details, because the magic of Versailles is inscribed in its geometry, numbers and measurements.

This knowledge has not been hidden from view. On the contrary, it's on display everywhere for anyone who wants to look. However, it has not been communicated openly either. We don't even point out that it exists; but anyone who suspects it's there will soon find clues to guide them. To demonstrate the validity of these assertions, I'll give an example that seems to have escaped everyone's notice.

## THE HUNDRED STEP STAIRCASE

To the south of the Parterre du Midi, in front of Louis XIV's château, lies the Orangerie. To get there, Louis XIV shows us the way:

*"We'll go down the right-hand ramp of the Orangerie and pass through the orange grove".*

What Louis calls the right-hand ramp is also known as the " 100 Step Staircase ". It is by this name that it is widely known. The top section can be seen in a 1695 painting (72) and a recent photograph shows its division into three sections separated by two landings (73).

For the diligent reader, it's possible to count the number of steps on the lower part of this photograph. There are 35. This is also the case for the other two sections, making a total of 105 steps.

In 2019, I had them counted by an acquaintance who has worked at the Château for over 15 years. He counted them going up and then a second time coming down. Stunned, he confirmed that he had counted 105 steps.

**The 100-step staircase actually has 105 steps!**

We can easily assume that the person who built the staircase knew there were 105 steps - the height was divided into 105 equal parts - but said nothing. For almost 350 years, no one seems to have counted them. It's a wonderful example of a well-kept secret that gives a numerical indication. But what is this indication?

The ratio of 100 to 105 can be reduced to 20:21. Between the "official" number and the announced one, we have increased by a twentieth part. This can be compared with the English guinea, a gold coin introduced in 1663, year when the Versailles Orangery was created, which was worth 21 shillings, compared with the pound, worth 20 shillings. Since the decimalisation of the English monetary system in 1971, the pound contains 100 pence and the guinea is worth 105 pence! When a price is advertised in guineas, it costs 5% more than the number would lead you to believe. You could call it the King's share!

In the second volume of this book, we'll discover that the geometry of the Versailles groves is based on a right-angled Pythagorean triangle, whose sides have the whole-number ratios of

$$20 : 21 : 29$$

The acute angle of this triangle is 43.6°. That's almost the diagonal angle of a square, 45°, but not quite. This is what makes the shape of the groves at Versailles so distinctive. But more on that later.

To conclude this first work, I'd like to give you the geometry of the main axis of Versailles, laid out from the outset by Louis XIII and his gardeners. I've already given you the angle, which is 21.8° north of the east-west axis.

**Now, 21.80° is half of 43.6°.**

(73) THE 100 STEPS ON THE WEST SIDE OF THE ORANGERIE *(Photo Copyleft)*

Axis of sunset on August 15
2
5

(74) The geometry of Versailles' main axis corresponds to a modular layout in relation to the cardinal axes of 2 by 5, whose diagonal gives an angle of 21.80° from the East-West axis. This angle is exact, and its correspondence with sunrise on November 1 and sunset on August 15 is quite remarkable. This astro-geometric principle only works at the latitude of Versailles.

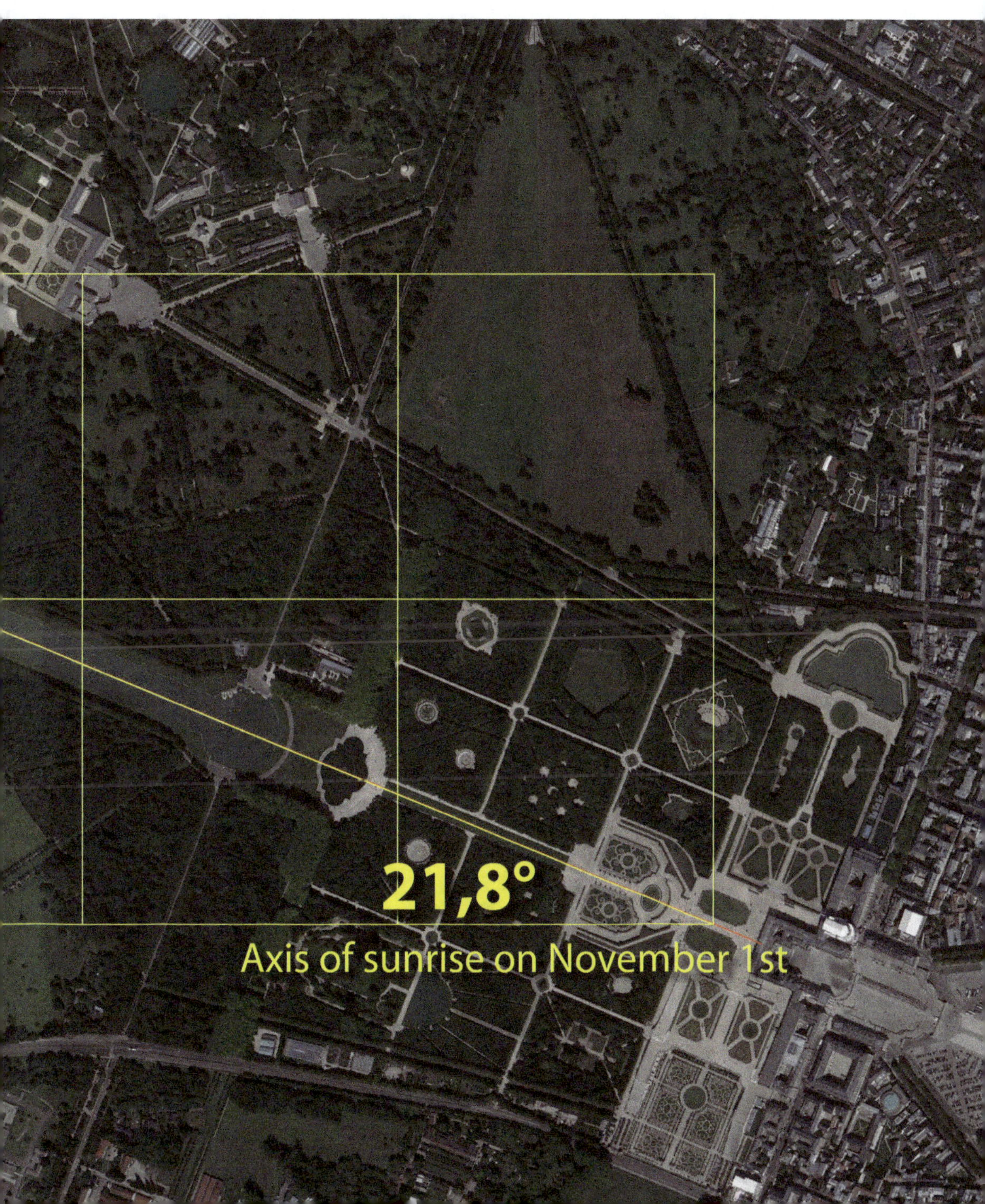

Although the orientation of the Val de Galie towards sunset on August 15 is already a remarkable fact, there is a simple geometry with whole numbers, laid out on the cardinal axes, which corresponds exactly to this direction. The combination of these two features in a single location gives it a truly exceptional character, in keeping with the ancient science I have named "astro-geometry", which is the application of two paths of the Quadrivium, geometry and astronomy.

The importance of the diagram (74) on the previous page cannot be underestimated.

It shows how the slope of the main axis of Versailles, in relation to the East-West axis, can be expressed by two integers, 2 and 5. In other words, to plot this slope, we need to draw 5 units of measure to the west and then two to the north.

This geometry is called "modular geometry" or "arithmetic layout" because it's based on modules, squares, which are positioned along the cardinal axes. It produces harmony through its use of whole numbers.

The numbers 2 and 5 in the Versailles landscape are two prime numbers in the Fibonacci series. This series of numbers, revealed by an Italian mathematician in the 15th century, was of paramount importance to ancient architects, as it tends towards the Divine Proportion, also known as the Golden Number or Phi. This proportion is 1 to 1.618 and is present in nature, in the positioning of leaves around a branch or seeds in the center of a sunflower, for example.

Everything points to the fact that behind the design of Versailles, the water features, gardens, bosquets, alleys... an ancient science is at work.

This will be the subject of the second volume.

# APPENDIX 1. EQUINOXES AND CARDINAL AXES.

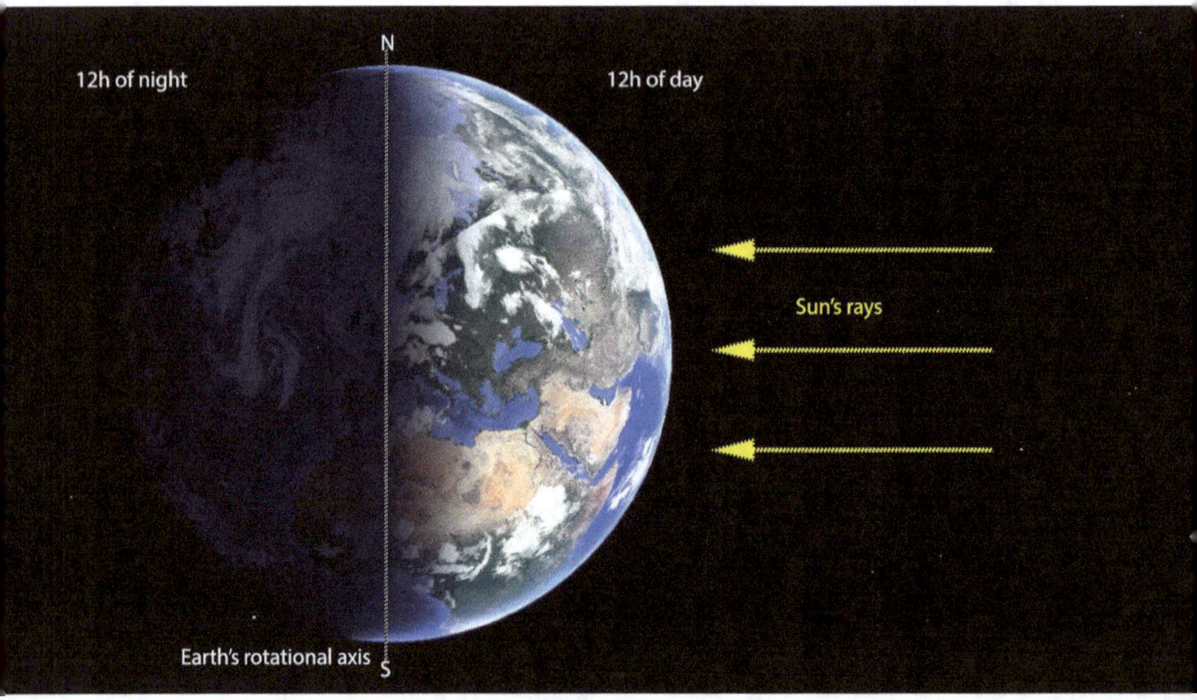

(75) The Earth seen from space at the moment of the spring equinox, when its axis is perpendicular to the Sun's rays.

(76) The marking of the equinox day on the El Castillo pyramid at Chichen Itza in Mexico attracts thousands of observers every year.

# Markers of the Year

Everyone knows that the Sun rises in the East and sets in the West. Fewer people, however, know that the Sun only rises exactly in the East at the time of the equinoxes, i.e. March 21 and September 23. On these days, people on the same north-south axis see the sun rise at the same moment. Everywhere on Earth, between the half Sun rising and setting at the horizon, there are 12 hours of day and 12 hours of night, hence the name equi-nox, equal nights (75).

This East-West axis corresponds to the center of the year-long movement of sunrise and sunset over the horizon. It is perpendicular to the north-south axis, which may seem obvious to us, but it is a major fact in the structuring of space and therefore of our current way of thinking. The omnipresence of the right angle in our modern world has its origins in the four cardinal axes, separated by 90°.

The equinox is defined as the moment when the earth's axis forms a right angle with the straight line connecting the center of the earth to the center of the sun. This is when the Earth's axis is perfectly aligned in the direction of its motion along its orbit. At the moment of the solstices, the Earth's axis is perpendicular to its movement around the Sun.

This division into four, the four seasons, is the division of 360° by 4, which is 90°. So, once we've established a north-south axis, a right-angled triangle allows us to determine the east-west axis.

It's around the equinoxes that the variation in daylight duration is greatest, at around 4 minutes per day at Paris latitude. As it rises above the horizon, the Sun moves by its own size every day; i.e. at the spring equinox, for example, where its left edge was the day before, its right edge will be the day after. Because of this non-negligible displacement, it is therefore very difficult to determine the East-West axis precisely by observing the sunrise at the moment of the equinoxes.

Mayan science has found a remarkable expression of this moment. At the El Castillo pyramid in Chichen Itza, Mexico, the Sun at sunset on the day of the equinox casts an undulating shadow of seven curves that seems to descend along the central staircase to form the body of the feathered serpent whose head is carved at the bottom of the staircase (76). Thousands of people gather every year to observe the phenomenon.

The Egyptians also went to great lengths to determine the exact day of the equinox. The north and south sides of the Great Pyramid are very slightly curved, so that when the sun rises exactly in the east, it simultaneously illuminates the two western edges of the monument. While the cardinal axes are not physically marked in the gardens of the Château de Versailles, their presence underpins the entire layout. No approximation is acceptable here.

# APPENDIX 2. EQUINOXES AND LATITUDES.

## LATITUDE MARKERS

It's at noon on the day of the equinox, when the Sun is exactly south and the shadow is north, that the latitude of a place can be easily determined by observing the shadow of a pillar. The ratio between the height of the pillar and the length of its shadow at that moment is called the co-latitude. From this ratio, it's easy to calculate the angle. By deducting this angle from 90°, we obtain the value of the latitude in degrees.

A ratio of whole numbers between a pillar and its shadow lends a special nature to latitude, which could be considered sacred.

This principle seems to have been inscribed in the Book of Genesis concerning the life of Abraham (Abram), the main patriarch of the Judaism, Christianity and Islam.

*Terah took Abram, his son, and Lot, son of Haran, son of his son, and Sarai, his daughter-in-law, wife of Abram, his son. They went out together from Ur of the Chaldees to the land of Canaan. They came as far as Haran, and lived there.[1]*

So Abraham left the ancient city of Ur, today in Iraq, which lies at latitude 30.96375°. Here, a 5-meter-high mast casts a shadow exactly 3 meters long at noon on the equinox (77).

Abraham travelled north-west along the Euphrates for over 925 km to the town of Charan, now Harran, in northern Syria at latitude 36.86989°. This city has a long history as a sacred site. In particular, it was the site of Islam's first university. The ruins of the mosque with its astronomical tower (78) still stand. Now, at this latitude, a 4-meter mast casts a 3-meter shadow. This ratio between the horizontal and vertical axis of 3 to 4 is reminiscent of Pythagoras' famous 3 4 5 triangle.

It's hard not to see in this story an indication of an ancient principle for determining sacred places.[2] Obviously, this way of thinking is far removed from today's considerations. We even allow ourselves to judge it as "primitive". We've lost sight of the fact that numbers are a universal language, totally free from cultural influence.

---

1       Genesis 11. 31

2       See my lectures on DVD, How the Ancients determined their sacred places, DVD's number 39, 40 and 41, Epistemea 2013

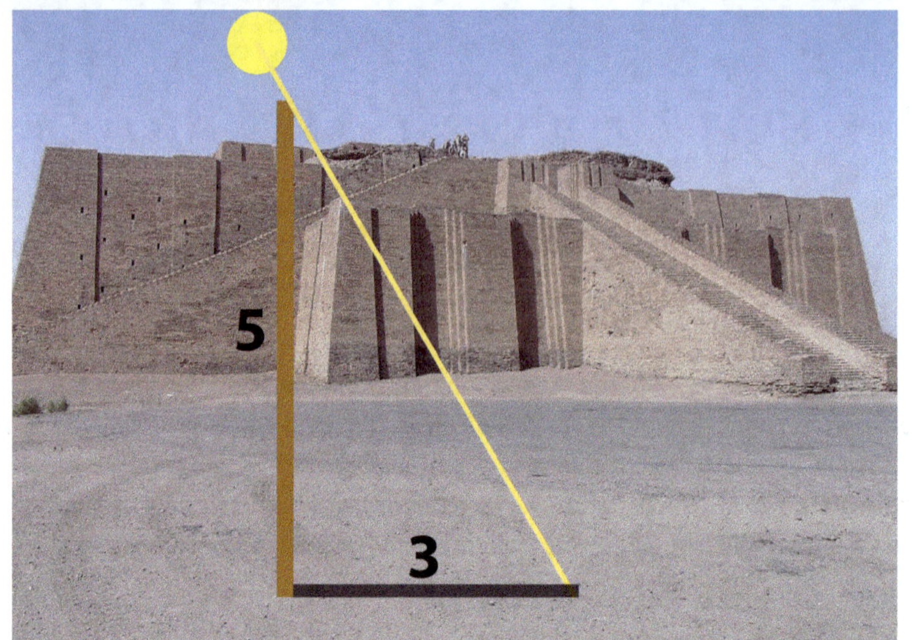


(77) THE RATIO BETWEEN THE HEIGHT OF A PILLAR AND THE LENGTH OF ITS SHADOW AT THE LATITUDE OF THE CITY OF UR IN CHALDEA (IRAQ) IS 5 TO 3. (LATITUDE 30.96375°)

(78) THE ASTRONOMICAL TOWER OF HARRAN IN SYRIA, (33.3M HIGH). AT NOON ON THE DAY OF THE EQUINOX, THE RATIO BETWEEN ITS HEIGHT AND THE LENGTH OF ITS SHADOW (WHICH EXTENDS DUE NORTH) IS 4 TO 3 (LATITUDE 36.86989°). THE SHADOW IS THEREFORE EXACTLY 25 METRES LONG.

Now, it would seem that these principles were not ignored in the choice of location for the Château de Versailles.

# APPENDIX 3. SOLSTICES

Starting on March 21 in the northern hemisphere, the sun rises further and further north of the east-west line, reaching its northern maximum on the day of the summer solstice. The orientation of this sunrise depends on latitude. The further north we are, the more the Sun is offset from the east-west axis. These four extreme positions of the Sun on the horizon (sunrise and sunset at summer and winter solstices) form a rectangle around the central observer.

For example, at the equator, the angle of sunrise at the solstice is 23° north of the east-west line.

At the latitude of Versailles, the offset is 38.05°.

On the same June 21, at latitude 67° above the Arctic Circle, the Sun descends to touch the horizon in the north, before rising again to start a new day. This is the famous midnight sun. Further north, it doesn't even set.

After the solstice, the rising sun moves south, returning to the East at the autumnal equinox. The sun then continues to rise further south until the winter solstice on December 21, the shortest day in the northern hemisphere. The offset from the East-West axis will be identical to that of the summer solstice, but this time to the south of this axis. The Sun's total amplitude at Versailles latitude will therefore be 38.05° x 2 or 76.1°. On this day, at noon on the Arctic Circle, the Sun makes a very brief appearance exactly to the south before night returns.

From this moment onwards, the days lengthen, the sunrises move northwards and we return to our starting point on March 21. As we have seen, this movement takes place on either side of the East-West line.

The word "solstice" comes from the Latin, "sol stare", meaning "the Sun stops". This is the moment of a change in direction, and for several days the Sun rises in virtually the same place. This moment of standstill at an extreme position was precisely marked in megalithic monuments as early as 5000 BC. Long, skilfully oriented corridors allowed the sun's rays to pass through only on the shortest days. The dolmen chamber received this solstice ray within, like a mystical seeding.

These extreme points in the annual cycle give each latitude its own particular geometry. The 4 points on the horizon positioned by sunrise and sunset at the summer and winter solstices form what is known as the latitude solstice rectangle. This shape changes very slightly over time, as the angle of inclination of the Earth's axis changes over a 41,000-year cycle. Since the Château de Versailles was built, the angle has changed by just 0.08 degrees.

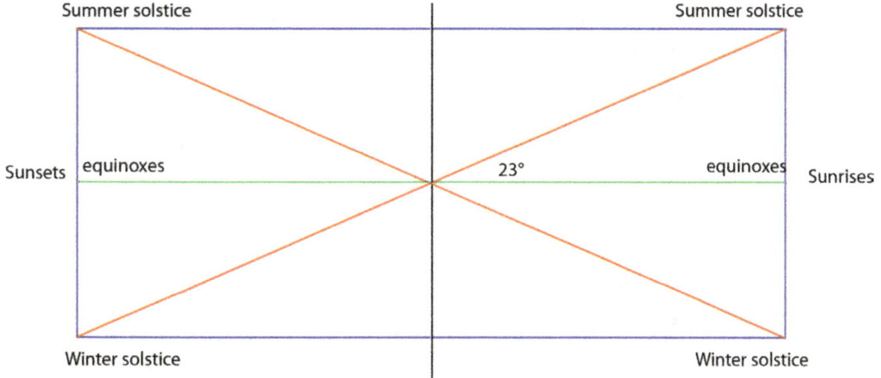



(79) SOLSTICE RECTANGLES FORMED BY THE POSITIONS OF EXTREME SUNRISES AND SUNSETS. ABOVE AT THE EQUATOR, BELOW AT VERSAILLES.

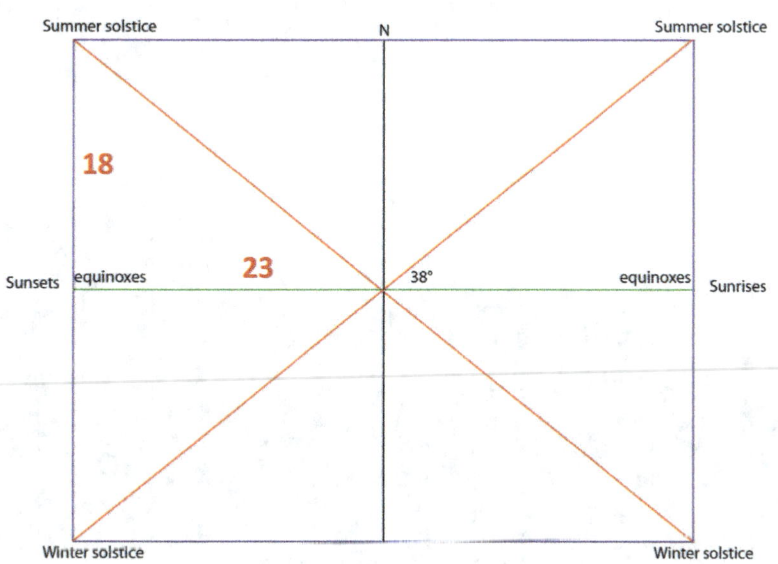

At certain latitudes and times, the solstice rectangle corresponds to simple geometry. This was the case for the Carnac megaliths in Brittany (the 3-4-5 triangle), but also for Karnak in Egypt (the double square or 1-by-2 rectangle).

At the latitude of Versailles, the solstitial angle of 38.05° gives a whole number ratio to the rectangle, 18 to 23.[3].

---

3        Atan(18/23) = 38.047°

(80) The sunrise ray arrives in the chamber of the Mane er Loh dolmen in Locoal-Mendon on the day of the winter solstice.

# INTERMEDIATE POSITIONS

Although the four positions of the Sun at the two solstices and two equinoxes are fundamental for framing space and time, as each position marks the beginning of a season[4], other intermediate axes could be of great importance. The most obvious of these are the positions that mark mid-season. But in the past, the position of the Sun at the beginning of each zodiac sign was also important.[5]

------

4        The winter solstice, the beginning of winter; the spring equinox, the beginning of spring; the summer solstice, the beginning of summer; and the autumn equinox, the beginning of autumn.

5        See my book *"La Science des Anciens" tome 1, Carnac, Le Menec,* éditions Epistemea 2015.

# Appendix 4. The Chartres diocese and Jean-François de Gondi

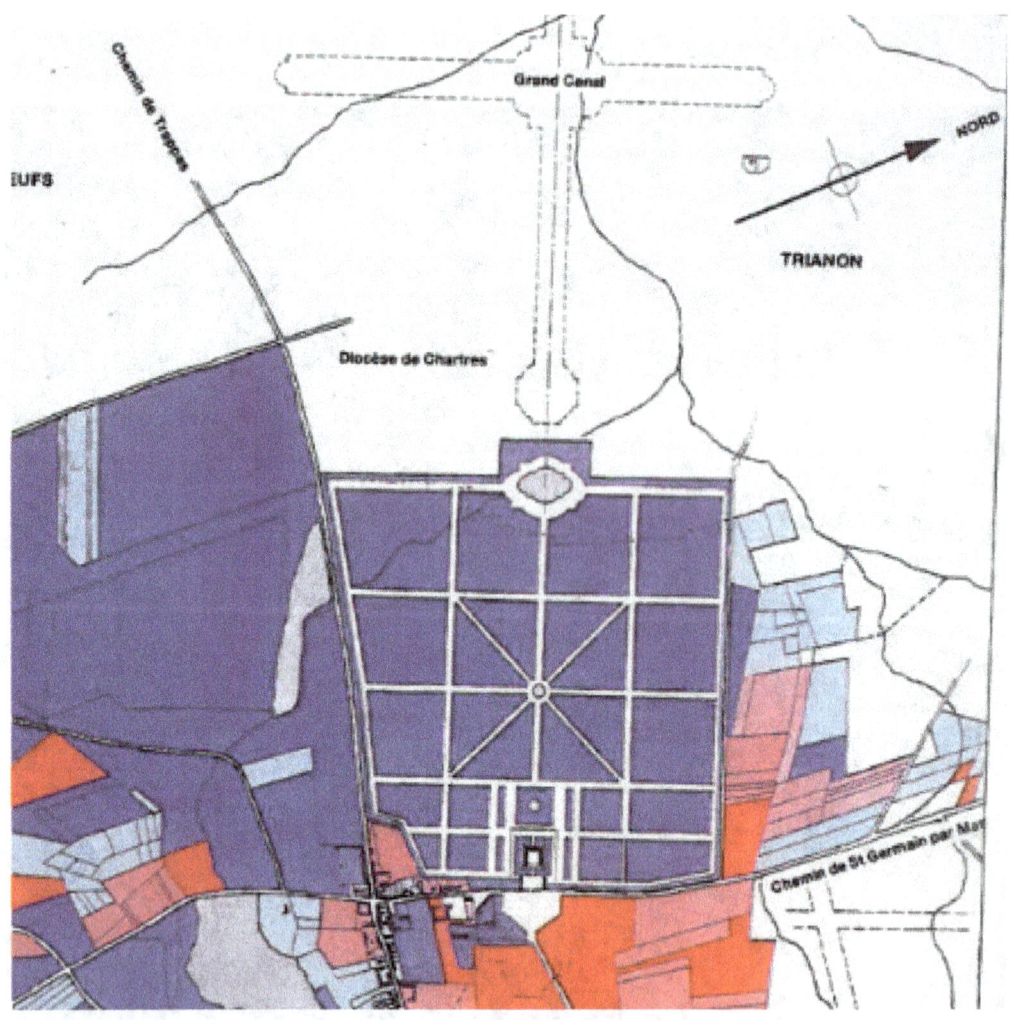


(81) Map of Versailles circa 1640, showing the site of the future Grand Canal fountain as part of the Diocese of Chartres.

The relationship between the druids and Chartres goes back a long way, as we saw in "Virgo Pariturae and the druids of Chartres", page 71. Now, part of the lands of Versailles, where the Grand Canal was to be built, belonged to the diocese of Chartres (81). In fact, the first mention of Versailles dates back to 1038, in a charter from the Abbey of Saint-Père in Chartres.

We have also seen that the builders of Chartres cathedral were already practicing astro-geometry when they constructed the present-day cathedral around 1200 (42). The orientation of their work was linked to the Virgin Mary, to whom they had dedicated the cathedral, Notre Dame de Chartres. There are several statues of the Virgin, including the Black Madonna of the Pillar, which is in the cathedral, and Our Lady Undergound, which is in the crypt, like the goddess Isis. It is highly likely that Louis XIII came to Chartres in 1637 on his tour of prayers to the Virgin Mary. On March 25, 1647, Louis XIV, then aged 8, came to Chartres with Anne of Austria. March 25 is the feast day of the Annunciation (commemoration of the announcement to the Virgin Mary of her maternity by the Archangel Gabriel, 9 months before December 25). This date therefore corresponded to the spring equinox.

We can only imagine what Anne of Austria felt on this occasion, as she became pregnant with her first child at the age of 37, following an intense program of national prayers to the Virgin.

The little château - a hunting lodge on the Versailles estate, where Louis XIII liked to go as early as 1621, was owned by Jean-François de Gondi. The lands surrounding the Domaine de Versailles belonged to the Saint-Julien de Versailles priory. In 1622, de Gondi was appointed to the bishopric of Paris, which until then had been under the archdiocese of Sens. On October 22 **of the same year**, Pope Gregory XV elevated the diocese of Paris to the rank of metropolitan archdiocese, with the **dioceses of Chartres**, Orléans and Meaux as suffragan dioceses. Jean-François de Gondi thus became the first archbishop of Paris, and the bishop of Chartres became subordinate to him. Moreover, the priory of Saint-Julien was hierarchically subordinate to the archbishop of Paris. There was therefore no obstacle to Louis XIII's taking possession of all the land necessary for the future settlement, as early as 1623[6].

Who was Jean-François de Gondi? He was born in Paris in 1584, the tenth and last child of Albert de Gondi, Duke Consort of Retz, and Claude Catherine de Clermont, Dowager Duchess of Retz and Baroness of Dampierre. His father is known to have been one of the main confidants of the Queen of France, Catherine de Médicis, in the 1570s,

---

6     However, he didn't officially buy them until 8 years later, on April 8, 1632.

at the moment of the Protestant massacres. It is said that he took advantage of this situation to buy Versailles for a pittance from Martial de Loménie, imprisoned for his Protestantism. Albert de Gondi went to see him in prison.

*In a dramatic scene, "using atrocious threats", he had him sign the sale of Versailles to him at a low price. Martial was nevertheless slaughtered in his prison on Saint Bartholomew's Day (August 24, 1572).[7]*

From 1616 to 1651, Jean-François de Gondi was commendatory abbot of Notre-Dame de la Chaume de Machecoul, where he introduced the reform of the Society of Brittany. His elevation to the rank of Archbishop of Paris is hard to fathom.

His nephew, Cardinal of Retz[8], calls him "very small-minded, and consequently jealous and difficult". He refers to "his negligence", his "incapacity", the " lowliness of his inclinations" and the " disturbance of his morals"..

*"The Archbishop of Paris, who was the weakest of all men, was, by a rather common process, the most glorious.... Though he talked like a linnet in private, he was always dumb as a fish in public." He had "little sense, and what little he had was not honest; he was weak and timid to the utmost extreme."*

It's rare to read such condemnation, especially from a man who is Archbishop of Paris. Was this man " hiding his cards "? Be that as it may, it was through his family and his position that the lands of Versailles were brought together to serve as the seat of one of the most beautiful palaces in the world.

The origins of the very first Lords of Retz remain unknown. They are traditionally said to have come from Brittany, as evidenced by Lord Harscoët's Breton-sounding first name. Pays de Retz is an area in the southwest of the Loire-Atlantique county in the Pays de la Loire region, which used to be part of Brittany.

Its name comes from the Latin Pagus Ratiatensis, "Pays de Rezé", the town of Rezé being its original port and capital. In ancient times, Rezé was known as Portus Ratiatus ("Port Ratiate"), Ratiatum Pictonum Portus ("Port des Pictons Ratiates"), Civitas Ratiatum ("City of the Ratiates"): The Ratiates were apparently a Picton sub-tribe. According to local historian Émile Boutin, the name Ratiates dates back to the 4th century B.C.,

---

7        https://fr.wikipedia.org/wiki/Martial_de_Lom%C3%A9nie

8        Édith Thomas, « *Chronologie du cardinal de Retz* », in Cardinal de Retz, Mémoires, coll. « Bibliothèque de la Pléiade », Gallimard, 1956

and derives from Phoenician merchants who sailed through the region to trade, notably on the nearby island of Noirmoutier. They would have named several places raas, which means "cape" in Hebrew, notably the cape of Pointe Saint-Gildas, which the sailors from Carthage had to sail around on their way to the Cassiterides islands, the tin islands. The word raas would later be used to designate what is now known as Pointe du Raz and Ras de Saint-Mathieu. It's an ancient and traditional country of historic Brittany, which became a barony and then a duchy. Its successive capitals were Rezé, then Pornic, and finally Machecoul from 1581.

# APPENDIX 5. DRUIDIC INFLUENCE AT VERSAILLES?

Many of the elements presented in this book lead us to suspect a Druidic influence on Louis XIII and Louis XIV. Could it be that Druid scholars had kept their knowledge alive through oral transmission over the centuries, and that the royal power lent them a receptive ear (82)?

Louis XIV's installation of the groves has a particularly Druidic connotation, as we know that the Druids gave their teachings in clearings in the middle of the groves. This is precisely how it was done at Versailles, with each grove containing its lesson in the form of a statue and staging.

There are other elements to support this idea. We have seen that the Druidic calendar divided the year into 9 months of 40 days each. Since the year represents a complete cycle or circle, we also understand that the division of the circle into 9 could be one of their emblems. A well-known Druid symbol is the triskel or triple spiral, which can be found engraved on megaliths at Newgrange in Ireland (83).

Other designs depict three Triskels nested in the heart of a circle, showing the division into 9, as can be seen at Strasbourg Cathedral (87).

Some embroideries still achieved in the Pays Bigouden near Quimper are table mats with the geometry of a circle divided into 9 parts. Now, in the Salon d'Apollon at the Château de Versailles, a detail caught my eye.

*The Salon d'Apollon was once the most sumptuous room in the entire grand apartment: it was first the King's bedroom before becoming the throne room. The ceiling is undoubtedly the masterpiece of Charles de la Fosse. In the center, Apollo on his chariot, accompanied by the figure of France and the procession of the seasons; in the corners, the allegories of the 4 continents[9].*

---

9    *Versailles, Château domaine collections*, Pierre Lemoine, 1991

Apollo is the god of light, driving the chariot of Helios, the Sun. From the 5th century B.C., the Greeks began to confuse him with Helios himself. He has a twin sister, Artemis in Greek or Diana in Roman, who is a lunar goddess. This obviously underlines the dual lunisolar nature of earthly life.

The chariot driven by Apollo on the ceiling of the Château de Versailles should clearly be understood as a solar chariot. Now, the detail that caught my attention was the fact that the chariot wheel is divided into 9 parts, in the manner of the Druids (84).

This can clearly be seen as an indication of the division of the solar year into nine, and would therefore subtly, but visibly, support the solar axes of Versailles. It's important to realize that we don't divide a circle into nine by accident or habit. Indeed, dividing a circle into 9 is a complex geometrical operation requiring intention. You can't draw the diameter because no point is opposite another.

The very name Apollo, whose etymology is obscure, may derive from Belenos, the Gallic god who evokes the light of the Sun. The Indo-European root bhel means "shining", "burning", "resplendent", "radiant" and gave its name to Baldr, god of light in Norse mythology, as well as to Bældæg, one of Odin's sons, and to Beli in Wales.

(83) ENTRANCE TO THE NEWGRANGE CAIRN IN IRELAND IN 1905, BEFORE ANY RESTORATION. A MAGNIFICENT TRISKEL (OR TRIPLE SPIRAL) IS ENGRAVED ON THE LEFT-HAND SIDE OF THE STONE.

Diodorus Siculus speaks of the existence of a people called the Hyperboreans, saying
they had been in contact with the Greeks since ancient times.

*"Beyond the land of the Celts, in the ocean, there is an island no smaller
than Sicily. This island, situated to the north, is, they say, inhabited by the
Hyperboreans, so called because they live beyond the point from which
Boreas blows[10]. The soil on this island is excellent, and so remarkably fer-
tile that it produces two harvests a year...*

*The island also boasts a vast enclosure dedicated to Apollo, as well as
a magnificent spherical temple adorned with numerous offerings... The
Hyperboreans speak a language of their own; they are very kind to the
Greeks, and particularly to the Athenians and Delians; and these sentiments
date back to ancient times. It is even claimed that several Greeks came
to visit the Hyperboreans, that they left rich offerings laden with Greek
inscriptions, and that Abaris, the Hyperborean, had once traveled to*

---

10      In Greek mythology, Boreas is the God of the North Wind.

(85) DETAIL OF APOLLO'S CHARIOT WITH ITS 9-SPOKE WHEEL.

*Greece to renew with the Delians the friendship that existed between the two peoples.*" [11]

The relationship between the ancient Celts and ancient Greece is not particularly well known to the general public.

---

11     Diodorus Siculus, Book II, 47–48

# GROTTE DE TÉTHYS

The Grotte de Téthys (named after the titanid Téthys, sister and wife of Ocean) is an artificial grotto built during the reign of Louis XIV in the lower part of a water tower, near the King's residence. Built in 1666 on the north side of the Château de Versailles, the grotto was adorned with three large marble sculptural groups representing Apollo bathed by nymphs and horses in the chariot of the Sun. The grotto was a key feature of the royal gardens, due to the symbolism it conveyed (the monarch being identified with the solar god Apollo) and the technical role it played in Versailles' water management. Destroyed in 1684, its sculpted groups are the only surviving reminder of this role.

According to Charles Perrault's memoirs, Perrault and his brother Claude, along with Le Brun, were commissioned to define the program for the grotto, based on a short passage from Ovid's Metamorphoses. The idea was to illustrate Apollo's resting place in the sea cave of the goddess Tethys, at the end of his diurnal journey.

While the idea for the grotto came from Louis XIV, Charles Perrault was responsible for the theme:

*« When the King had ordered the Versailles grotto to be built, I thought that, since His Majesty had taken the Sun as his motto, (...) it would be a good idea to use Apollo, who goes to bed with Thetis after having circumnavigated the earth, to represent that the King who comes to rest at Versailles after having worked to do good for the world. »*

This enchanting place, which marked the most festive years of Versailles, made La Fontaine say :

*"When the Sun is weary, and has completed his task, He descends to Thetys, and takes some respite: Thus Louis goeth to relax."*

Madame de Scudéry succumbs to the visitor's enchantment:

*"The eyes are delighted, the ears are charmed, the mind is astonished, and the imagination is overwhelmed (...)"*

Gaspard and Balthazar Marsy's Horses of the Sun, groomed by tritons, are on the left. Carved from a single block of Carrara marble, they illustrate the horses' vesper rest after Apollo's diurnal race. A force of nature in its raw state, animal instinct is opposed

(86) Apollo's Grove. (statues moved from the Grotte de Téthys).

to the measure and self-control of the god who reigns over the order of the world.

*"The Grotte de Téthys was part of a general garden design scheme, in which the solar theme was to mark the main axis, with the Apollo and Latona fountains, begun in 1668 [12]".*

12      Alexandre Maral, *Le Bosquet des Bains d'Apollon*, dans L'Estampille-L'Objet d'art, n°457, mai 2010, pp. 48-55

(87) The triple triskel in a window at Strasbourg Cathedral.

Howard Crowhurst moved to the Carnac area in 1985 and has been studying megaliths ever since. In 1989, he directed his first film, a 40-minute documentary about Carnac. He has taken part in several major French TV documentaries on Carnac and in 2010, he appeared on the British TV show Coast. In 2017, he took part in a documentary for What on Earth on Discovery Channel. He was a speaker at the Megalithomania conference in England in 2009, 2011, 2017 and 2021. Since 2006, with the ACEM association, he has organized the Summer Solstice event in Carnac (megalithes.info@gmail.com), bringing together speakers from around the world.

In December 2023 his latest full-length feature film, « Megaliths, forgotten world «, a fictional account of the discovery of Carnac by a couple of city dwellers, will be released. He has written eleven books on his research into the science of the Ancients, published by Epistemea, six of which are available in English, plus a little Wooden Book called Carnac. His book, «Carnac, the alignments», has received rave reviews. Professor Robert Temple wrote: «This is the most brilliant analysis of a megalithic site in the history of archaeology». Howard has also recorded over 50 lectures, available on Internet and DVD. He can be contacted through his publisher at epistemea@gmail.com